INSIDE THE MIND OF A KILLER

INSIDE THE MIND OF A KILLER

ON THE TRAIL OF FRANCIS HEAULME

Jean-François Abgrall

with

Samuel Luret

Translated by Ros Schwartz

P

PROFILE BOOKS

First published in Great Britain in 2004 by
PROFILE BOOKS LTD
58A Hatton Garden
London EC1N 8LX
www.profilebooks.co.uk

First published in France in 2002 by
Albin Michel
www.albin-michel.fr

10 9 8 7 6 5 4 3 2 1

Printed and bound in Great Britain by
Bookmarque Ltd, Croydon, Surrey

ISBN 1 86197 656 9

Liberté · Égalité · Fraternité
RÉPUBLIQUE FRANÇAISE

Author's note

For the purpose of this book, the investigation is described in chronological order. However, only the statements, reports and miscellaneous documents made public during the court hearings have been used.

Translator's note

It may help the reader to know that in France there are two police forces, the Police and the gendarmerie. The Police operate in cities, and the gendarmerie, which is a military structure, in rural areas. Under French law, serious cases are referred to an investigating magistrate, the *juge d'instruction*, who takes formal charge of the investigation. He or she determines which witnesses are to be called, and will hear evidence from the witnesses and the suspect before the trial.

To all those who believed in and assisted
with these investigations.

PART ONE

Pursuit

Moulin Blanc Beach

Sunday 14 May 1989 was one of those long sunny days that make being on duty even more tedious, particularly as that weekend was the culmination of a stressful week for the Rennes gendarmerie's criminal investigation unit.

The offices were deserted, the telephones silent. Time plodded by, punctuated only by trips to the coffee machine and the radio operations room to collect the occasional fax. There was nothing earth-shattering: a few sporadic burglaries in different parts of Brittany that would have to be investigated to see if there were any links, notifications of arrests for car thefts, brawls and two or three flashers. The warm weather often brings them out of the woodwork.

To relieve the monotony, I reread various documents and planned my forthcoming trips. I had to go to Nantes to take part in a series of arrests in a drug-trafficking case. Then, if all went

well, I would go on to Saint Brieuc, where the local gendarmerie had asked for our help in investigating a series of armed
robberies. The day wore on.

5.10 p.m.: an urgent telex. A murder had just been committed on Moulin Blanc beach, at Le Relecq-Kerhuon, just outside
Brest. Aline Pérès, aged forty-nine, had been stabbed. Her body
had been found lying in the middle of the beach by passers-by.
Lying in the middle of the beach ... Odd. I knew that beach
well. I had lived in the area for nearly five years. It was a quiet
place where nothing ever happened, where families went for a
stroll, especially on Sundays. A strange place for a murder.

That was all the message said. I needed more information.
Most homicides committed in the region were handled by our
division. I would probably be put in charge of the investigation.

I called the local gendarmes. We often worked together. The
year before, we had collaborated over the murders of a company
boss and an oyster farmer. The officer on duty had very few
details. He informed me that several teams were already at the
scene.

5.15 p.m.: Joseph, nicknamed 'Jop', my partner at that time,
was nowhere to be found. Head of the Rennes mobile delin-
quency squad, he was fluent both in Breton and the language of
the gypsies. A few weeks away from retirement and anticipating
an uneventful spell on duty, he had decided to take a little trip to
south Finistère, to see some 'intelligence agent' known only to
him. He had gone off without leaving a contact number. I got
the message.

The Commander's Peugeot 305 was the best available vehicle. We were routinely assigned old cars as apparently we spent too much time on the road. The advantage was that it was grey and could always be used as an unmarked vehicle.

I drove fast. The 200 kilometres sped by. If the old traffic cops saw me, they'd come out with their usual clichés – 'Slow down, death will wait, take it easy …' But I knew speed was the essence. An investigation is a time-machine for going backwards. The murderer had been in the vicinity of the beach around 5 p.m. I had to be there as fast as possible before vital evidence was lost. Clues are often short-lived.

6.50 p.m. The road took me right to the beach car park. The place is popular with windsurfers all year round, in all weather, a busy beach, over a kilometre long, where walkers pause to gaze at the sea, where people like to stroll, and children come to swim. Bordered by one of the roads into Brest, its sandy stretches unfurl in a leisurely fashion from the Moulin Blanc marina to the Sables Rouges headland. Near the car park there's a pebble beach. I knew that this less savoury section was not frequented by the same beachgoers as the sandy part. Older people liked to come here to avoid mocking stares when they put on their swimsuits. It was quieter here, and the regulars knew each other by sight.

Despite the holiday atmosphere created by the spring sunshine, I was aware of the murder scene nearby. Soon I spotted the gendarmerie's vehicles and recognised several colleagues. The victim's body was still lying on the beach, covered with a white sheet. It looked abandoned, lying parallel to the sea, as if by mistake. I noticed signs of a struggle being carelessly trampled by a gendarme. I hoped they'd been photographed. Other clues were vanishing under my eyes: bystanders were beginning to amble off into the distance without having been identified.

I quickly examined the body. The victim was a small woman of around fifty, with short, light-brown hair. She was lying on her back, her legs straight and her arms by her sides. There was grit clinging to her right cheek. She was wearing only the bottom half of a bikini. I was struck by the grisly wound to her throat, though there was surprisingly little blood. Her throat had been slit from the middle to behind the left ear. It was a 'clean' wound, sharp and precise. There were other stab wounds to the heart and at the base of her spine where the marks from the hilt of the weapon were still visible. The suddenness and brutality of the attack were unusual. It had the air of an execution, an explosion of violence. I looked around, scanning the area for vital clues.

It was too incongruous, crazy even, to kill on a Sunday afternoon on this packed beach. Had this spot, which I knew so well, changed? Or was it the crime that was out of place? And who was this woman?

My colleagues' activity broke into my thoughts. Each person concentrated on his job: mug shots, fingerprints and IDs of curious onlookers drawn to the scene. The atmosphere was tense, heavy. Sheer disbelief was visible on every face.

The victim's belongings were a few metres away, resting against the sea wall. I looked carefully. The marks on the ground pointed to the presence of another person. Did a bloodstain near the towel necessarily indicate the start of the attack? All around, the little flat pebbles had been disturbed, trampled, but there had not been any big movements. Two identical deep imprints indicated to me that Aline Pérès had knelt down. Car keys protruded from her jeans pocket. Nobody leaves their keys lying around on a beach. The victim had probably been trying to grab them. And those other blood stains … They started by her bag and continued less visibly to the position where the body lay. This woman had been helpless. Each thrust had hit home. The murderer was precise, experienced … I had the impression it was the act of a madman, but committed consciously. A cold-blooded killing.

I joined the team at the edge of the beach. The lieutenant supervising the investigation was summing up the facts. 'The victim has been identified. She's a nurse from Brest.' Then he expounded his theory on how the murder had been carried out. He could already picture the whole thing. 'After being attacked unexpectedly from behind, the victim crawled a few metres. The murderer stabbed her first in the back, then in the heart and lastly he slit her throat …'

How could he be so sure? The expressions on the faces of some of the seasoned officers spoke volumes.

On these initial military conclusions, they were asked to meet at the local gendarmerie to set up an incident room. The lieutenant was in a hurry. He had two objectives: to inform his superiors as soon as possible and to arrest the murderer in record time. His hectic activity betrayed a state of agitation that can often be contagious.

In the lobby, witnesses were waiting to give statements. Many of them lived near the scene of the crime. Among them was a short, shy-looking man of around fifty, sitting in a corner, looking ill at ease and quite distraught. Nobody was taking any notice of him. I went over. He told me that he was married and that he had known the victim for years. 'I was with her last night. What happened?' he asked me.

'We're going to take care of you,' I told him.

At that point, an officer appeared and announced that everyone would have to wait a little longer.

As it turned out, the witnesses were interviewed immediately, without any precautions or any real detachment. They would probably all have to be questioned again. The witnesses were party to the constant coming and going of the officers; they overheard the radio communications and the various conversations of the teams returning from the beach. There was no discretion. The twenty investigators who had been brought in were rushing around in all directions. With the help of Bertrand from the local gendarmerie and François, the head of the Brest criminal investigation unit, I gently tried to calm things down.

8.30 p.m.: the end of the first case review. Now we had to organise the teams and put the right people in place. We entrusted the most important checks to the steadiest, most experienced officers, who wouldn't be discouraged if they failed to obtain immediate results. Everybody had a particular line of inquiry to pursue. We seemed to have struck a balance between emergency measures and background investigation. After talking to the Brest substitute public prosecutor, I was put in charge of the case.

Experience has shown that the beginning of an investigation is the most crucial time. It is vital not to omit anything or to rush into things, even though sometimes it is tempting to dive straight in. Details overlooked can never be retrieved.

The first task was to find new witnesses. Maps of the district were issued. One by one, the residents were methodically questioned. We passed on the information to the Brest police. The fire service, hospitals, taxis and all-night bars were alerted. None of the team got any sleep that night, but by dawn there was little to show for their efforts. There was not a single eyewitness account.

9 a.m., Monday 15 May 1989. Everybody looked tired, but they battled on. It is not unusual to have so little to show after only one day of inquiries. During a criminal investigation, we proceed first of all by elimination, exploring every possible avenue, starting with the list of the most recently released convicts, arrivals of injured patients in the hospitals, and reports of stolen vehicles. Refuse collection in the vicinity of the beach had been suspended in case the murder weapon was in one of the bins. All the manholes in the area were also examined one by one. Records of all calls made from the public telephones on the beach were requested and the numbers traced. Somewhere there had to be a witness, a clue ... We followed up every lead. I found it hard to believe that a woman could be murdered on a beach, in the middle of the afternoon, without anybody seeing or hearing a thing. I returned to the scene with Bertrand and

tried shouting. My cries were drowned by the noise of the waves and the traffic. They couldn't even be heard sixty metres away. But was that really an answer?

In the space of a few hours, numerous interviews had taken place. They only seemed to add to the mystery. All the evidence confirmed that the beach had been far from empty at the time of the murder.

The first glimmer of hope came in the early afternoon. One of my close colleagues returned to the gendarmerie accompanied by a man from Brest, around sixty years old, sturdy and athletic, a regular from the beach. They shut themselves in one of the offices, where I joined them.

A first crucial testimony. 'On Sunday, I was sunbathing about a hundred metres from the victim,' the witness told us. 'I walked past her when I arrived at the beach and even said hello before choosing a spot further on. At 5 p.m. she was alive, I'm certain. I was watching her while I listened to the finish of a horse race on the radio.'

He even remembered that at that point two men had been walking towards her. 'They were shabbily dressed, but not dirty, they weren't tramps. I can't give you a precise description because I had the sun in my eyes,' he explained.

He told us apologetically that he had turned his head the other way to hear the radio more clearly, and stayed like that until the police arrived.

'A boy of around twelve wearing fluorescent green was playing on the beach, between the victim and myself,' he volunteered at the close of the interview.

The call to the fire brigade had been logged at 5.04 p.m. Thanks to the evidence we had just heard, the time of the murder had now been established. We decided to appeal for witnesses through the press. With a bit of luck, the amateur photographers and video enthusiasts who were on the beach that Sunday would give us more useful clues. Perhaps someone had caught the murderer on camera.

5 p.m. I was given the backup of two colleagues from Rennes, Jean-Claude and Jean-Paul. These two were tough, top-level professionals, hard-boiled characters forged by years of experience. Their presence was reassuring. They had given me vital help in the past, in a hold-up case. Their arrival couldn't have been more timely.

The journalists had been on our heels for several hours and we were under mounting pressure. Not everything was to be made public; but there had been a number of leaks.

I prompted the two investigators to find out everything they could about the victim. Her work life, her love life and her family, everyone she knew, friends or otherwise. We retraced her day-to-day movements, found out about her hobbies and her tastes, delved into her preferences and her passions ... We explored every facet of her personality. Uncovering a victim's private life is a delicate, sometimes unsettling, task. It is hard to pry into a person's secrets without it affecting both their relatives and the investigators. But that is a crucial part of the investigation. Knowing the victim well would give us a much better chance of finding out what had happened on the day of the murder.

My job was to handle the forensic analyses. Aline Pérès's car, a little blue Ford Fiesta, had been taken to the gendarmerie garage. Nobody had touched it yet. The CARME private laboratory on the outskirts of Brest used advanced technology that the gendarmerie didn't have. I called up one of the technicians. He used the Polylight technique which projects light frequencies that reveal normally invisible evidence such as fluids and fibres. In total darkness, he swept the bodywork of the vehicle. We wore strange welder's goggles that enabled us to see various different marks appear, as if by magic. Fingerprints and dust began to glow. Inside the car, the fluorescent fibres from passengers' clothing could be distinguished from the fabric of the seat. They looked huge. Stray hairs became valuable clues. Cigarette butts were gathered up and sealed in bags. A sample of dust was taken from the floor. It could be compared to samples taken from the shoes of a suspect.

I felt heartened by these micro-samples. The clothing fibres gave me a description of the passengers' clothing, the colour of their trousers and shirts … It was encouraging.

They were added to the samples taken on the beach from under the victim's fingernails. Had she scratched her attacker? Did we know the killer's blood group? It was still too early to tell, but these were the first clues.

16 May 1989, the date of the autopsy at the Kerfautras forensic medical institute in Brest – not an attractive place. At 2 p.m. the

procession of investigators and magistrates crossed the huge cemetery giving access to the morgue. We were shown into a small room with a high ceiling. There were about ten of us standing round the metal table on which the victim's body lay. The only sound was the tinkling of the coroner's instruments. There was a general awkwardness; everybody avoided looking at the body, their eyes drawn instead to the wall charts informing us of the average weight of a man's liver, or that of a woman's or a child's brain. And yet there was something powerful about the presence of this body, as if it held the key to the mystery.

Aline Pérès had graduated from victim to prime witness.

Methodically, the coroner examined every mark, every detail, and explained them. He was surprised at the violence and precision of the stab wounds. The main injuries were on the neck, the sternum and the lower back. Right from the start the one on the neck had caught my attention, but the doctor told me that it hadn't been fatal. The wounds showed that the weapon used was very sharp. The coroner noted a slight abnormality in these cuts. He inferred that they had been made by a small knife with a damaged blade. The victim had not put up much of a struggle. She had died from a blow to the heart. In addition to the stab wounds, I was surprised to see three scratch marks on the neck.

I tried to imagine the grip ... It was difficult, and I said so to the coroner. He slowly moved his hand and superimposed his fingers over the marks. With his other hand, he mimed the action of the knife, imitating the movements of the murderer. I was gradually able to visualise the scene. The murderer had grabbed Aline Pérès under the chin with his left hand, and slit her throat with his right hand. So he had stood facing her. This movement was surprising: the attacker had twisted his left hand over, the thumb facing outwards, to grab his victim's neck. As a result, his fingerprints were reversed. An extremely unusual hold. I had never seen such a movement. I knew at once that the murderer was not a run-of-the-mill criminal. And finally the coroner pointed out that the little bruise on the top of her forehead was the result of a blow from a very tall person.

The examination ended with samples being taken for anatomical and pathological tests. There we were, faced with all the available data.

Samples were also taken from the victim's wounds. They probably contained particles of metal from the murderer's knife. To find out, I travelled to the village of Plouvorn, a few kilometres from Brest, where there is a small electron microscope laboratory. Through circumstance, this place had become our local crime institute. The technician showed me into a tiny room full of equipment where the human tissue was taken out of the sealed bags with extreme caution to avoid contamination.

Under the electronic eye of a scanning microscope, the samples yielded their secret in less than half an hour. The murderer's knife was made of iron, pure iron, no alloy. It was a simple blade, not chromium-plated or treated. That immediately eliminated throwing knives, fighting knives and professional chef's knives. This was useful information.

There was a man who could perhaps help me narrow down my search: the gunsmith at the bottom of Rue de Siam, in Brest.

The bladed weapons were displayed on the back wall of his shop, between the gun rack and the boxes of pistols. There were knives and daggers of all kinds, all of them deadly. Instinctively, I pictured the murder weapon among them.

'You're looking for a knife with an iron blade?' he asked in surprise. 'Look in the display case to your right.'

To my surprise, he was pointing to a range of Opinel knives, plain knives with wooden handles and a metal ring to lock the blade. These 'little knives' did not look dangerous, and I said so. The dealer then picked one up at random, opened out the blade and slowly cut a sheet of paper, as if with a razor.

He added, 'These are the only knives with an iron blade that you'll find on the market.'

Was the murder weapon such a humdrum object? I felt dubious.

9 p.m. Back at the gendarmerie in Le Relecq-Kerhuon, we held a review. We sat in the main room. It was hard to fit everyone in. I summed up the results of the tests and my visit to the gunsmith, and then it was Jean-Claude and Jean-Paul's turn to report on their day. They had been to Brest regional hospital where the victim used to work. They were already calling her Aline, as if they had known her well. This is common among investigators who get involved in the subject's life. The evidence of her colleagues and of the director of the hospital was unequivocal: they all declared that Aline Pérès had been an excellent nurse. She was calm and energetic, and had worked in casualty for several years. She was used to emergencies and knew exactly how to handle them. A woman of experience then, not easily caught unawares. And yet …

A third investigator went on:

'A man telephoned in answer to the appeal for witnesses in the press. He'd photographed some boats in the marina at 5 p.m. He didn't see anything, but came forward just in case.'

Of no apparent interest, but who could tell? Another team signalled a stabbing that had taken place on the evening of the murder, near Brest castle. The victim, a man of around forty, had his face badly slashed with a knife. The attacker, a stranger, had fled. The wounded man was currently being treated at the naval hospital. Look into that.

Other information had been gathered by the rest of the team: the site of the murder was a popular haunt of junkies and vagrants, and a few local voyeurs and flashers who tended to hang out on this beach had been identified.

Faced with this wealth of information, we decided to interview all the drifters as a matter of urgency. Jean-Claude and Jean-Paul were given reinforcements and detailed to go and interview the Pérès family. Meanwhile, I was to meet the three people who had discovered the body, a fifty-two-year-old woman and her adult son and daughter who had come to lunch that Sunday.

'After coffee,' she explained, 'we decided to go for a little walk, it was such a lovely day. The Sables Rouges headland is pleasant and it's sheltered from the wind. Besides, it's not far from our house.'

Offering a spectacular panoramic view of the port of Brest, the headland was easily accessible. They had set out at 4.45 p.m., making their way among the rocks, unwittingly approaching the scene of the murder 600 metres away. It was the woman's twenty-year-old son who remembered the most details. He had probably not been paying attention to his mother and sister's conversation. In any case, he clearly recalled the woman of around fifty who was sunbathing in a secluded spot between two rocks, well hidden from view.

'Then I noticed a man, of around fifty,' he went on. 'He was wearing a thong. When we walked past him, he got up and went for a swim. Then a boy aged about twelve or fourteen arrived alone. He was wearing fluorescent green shorts and a T-shirt. He stopped to play in a rock pool.'

'Then what?'

'As we neared the car park I noticed two people lying down. The first was a man listening to a transistor radio. The second, a woman, aroused my curiosity. She was lying the wrong way to sunbathe. Then I looked at my mother and sister. We all had the same thought. We went up to her and that's when we discovered the body covered in blood. We immediately called the police from the phone booth nearby. It was four minutes past five.'

This was a valuable lead, even though it didn't tell us anything about the two men other witnesses had seen near Aline Pérès at 5 p.m. I noted that in fact there hadn't been many people on that side of the headland. Perhaps the murderer had scrambled up the rocky slope and fled along the coast road.

I hoped that the photos taken from the jetty would bring me more specific answers. Bertrand had traced the amateur photographer.

'He's certain he used his camera at 5 p.m.,' he told me, 'he remembers looking at his watch.'

I examined the photos, but there was nothing very exciting.

Clearly, there were key witnesses at either end of the beach at the time of the murder, but none of them was looking in the right direction. In spite of everything, we were determined to get these photos to speak. The negatives measured 2.4 by 3.6 centimetres.

A photographic laboratory in Le Relecq-Kerhuon offered us the use of an enlarger and we spent the evening projecting the negatives. One by one, we pored over each shot. Only number six was of interest. It showed a corner of the Sables Rouges headland, but from so far away ... It was probably unusable.

The lab technician offered to work on that part of the negative, which was about a quarter of the size of a postage stamp. The next day, an A3 format enlargement was on our desk. The amorphous mass of coloured pixels bewildered us. It was hard to make out the objects but we tried to interpret this fuzzy picture once our eyes had grown accustomed to it. With the aid of a magnifying glass, we managed to identify the witnesses present on the beach.

The three little splodges side by side, a mix of grey, green and yellow, were the three people who had found the body, the mother and her son and daughter. The white patch with two red lines was the woman sunbathing. The boy in fluorescent green was there too. We also pinpointed the man in swimming trunks and the witness listening to the radio. Gradually, Moulin Blanc beach emerged as it had been at the time of the crime. Unfortunately, the photo stopped just before the place where the victim was, and, fatally, her murderer. We were bitterly disappointed. For the time being, Aline Pérès's murderer kept his secret.

Over the next few days the first people were brought in for questioning. There were several squats around Moulin Blanc beach. Vagrants, junkies and the sexual deviants who hung around with them were interviewed. A fringe world full of weird characters, like the flasher dressed in the traditional raincoat and a pair of trousers cut off halfway up his thigh and held up solely by two pieces of string acting as braces.

These leads soon petered out – the interviewees wanted to be helpful, but they had nothing new to tell us. The incident prompted many of them to up and leave. We set off in pursuit. We soon put names and then faces to the transient population of Moulin Blanc beach.

A few checks on hostels for the homeless enabled us to track down these witnesses one by one. We worked fast, but many of them had lost all sense of time. Sometimes, their conversation would take a worrying turn, like that of a man nicknamed Cheyenne.

'Since I got out of prison, I haven't been near Moulin Blanc ... I do carry a penknife which I use for eating. I also carry a Stanley knife. I found it in a squat. So far, I've only used it to cut the bottoms off Sparrow's trousers because he's got his leg in plaster.'

The knife in question did not have a nick in it and was not made solely of iron. Another red herring.

The statements of two other vagrants finally led us to the

Emmaüs hostel* on the clifftop at Le Relecq-Kerhuon, just a few hundred metres from Moulin Blanc beach. The stretch of beach where Aline Pérès's body had been found was a popular haunt of the homeless from the Emmaüs community. This information corroborated local people's statements. Accompanied by a colleague, I paid the community a visit. It was a large property, surrounded by a high grey concrete wall. It was impossible to get inside without being seen by the porter sitting in reception. The director made his way across the little garden towards us. Introductions were rapidly made. He seemed quite relieved to see us.

'Everybody here was shocked by the incident too, and several members of the community wanted to leave the day after the murder. They didn't want to come into contact with the police and become suspects.'

That was understandable, but it didn't help.

'Besides, on 14 May, most of them were out of the area, they'd gone to an inter-community meeting in another town. Only the sick, the elderly and the new arrivals stayed here. Twelve people in all,' he added. 'Now there are only two of them left in our community.'

We asked to see them. The two men who joined us had closed-up faces that bore the scars of the hard lives they had led.

Watching them walk, I recalled the description of one of the witnesses, *'They were shabbily dressed, but not dirty, they weren't tramps.'* The men told us how they had spent their Sunday. In

---

* Translator's note: Equivalent of the Salvation Army.

the early afternoon, they had sat in the dining room, watching TV, the smaller man began. Everything was quiet, but then, around 4.30, a fight broke out between two men. Others got involved. The men had to be separated before somebody got hurt. Some even went out to cool off ...

I found this extremely interesting. I had the feeling that here was something tangible, that might have some bearing on the murder. Homeless men, some armed with knives. People fired up from a fight that had broken out on this first warm day. The hostel located a few hundred metres from the scene of the murder. And all those hasty departures ...

The names of these witnesses, all potential suspects, were listed in the hostel's records. We sent out wanted notices all over France. I already knew it would be several weeks before we heard anything.

In the meantime, we finished following up local leads. It was now the end of May. This time we targeted the drug dealers. Brest had become a major heroin trafficking centre, involving several gangs. Fanch, the head of the drugs squad at Brest police station, was an old friend of mine. He told me that dealing sometimes went on at Moulin Blanc. He thought that the irrational nature of the attack could be the act of a junkie in withdrawal. We decided to pool our efforts.

Within a few days the arrest count shot up, and in less than a week the local dealers started sending us messages. They were worried by our joint action. The street price of drugs had never been so high, and the goods were in short supply. They wanted us to find the killer and even offered us their services. If they found out anything, they would let us know … But they came up with nothing.

This slow progress demoralised the fainter-hearted. Some investigators already believed we would never identify the murderer, particularly because their presence in the police stations was causing friction. The identikit picture of the knife attacker near Brest castle on the evening of the murder on the beach was pinned up on the wall in every office in the station. The police were looking for a thin-faced suspect aged around thirty, with long fair hair drawn back off his face and a clear gaze. Supposing he was our man too? they thought. Two gendarmes were tasked with following that line of inquiry. They too drew a blank.

Beginning of June. It would soon be the summer holidays and the investigation was floundering. I dreaded the summer. It's a time when everything grinds to a halt. A real obstacle to thorough investigations.

But then a fourteen-year-old boy rekindled our hopes. The appeal for witnesses in the press at last bore fruit. On 8 June, Philippe walked into the gendarmerie of Le Relecq-Kerhuon, accompanied by his father.

'I'm the boy in the fluorescent green shorts,' he began.

Resting his elbows on the corner of a little desk, this fragile-looking young man spoke. He had gone for a walk along the beach before settling near the sunbathing woman at around 4.45 p.m. He had stayed there for around ten minutes, sitting on a concrete slab. A little embarrassed, he admitted he had been attracted by the woman's bare breasts. On becoming aware of his presence, she had discreetly put her top back on. But there was also a man standing there, on top of the rocks about thirty metres away. He stood upright, like a lookout, not far from the road. His hair was dishevelled and he was overdressed for the time of year. From his vantage point, the individual, who was aged about forty, could see right across the Sables Rouges area.

Philippe had then set off for the rocky headland. I couldn't help thinking that he had unwittingly just sealed Aline Pérès's fate. His departure was the moment the killer had been waiting for.

2

The first meeting with Francis Heaulme

16 June 1989. It is said that the murderer always returns to the scene of the crime, but in my experience they have always tended to hare off in the opposite direction. Despite that, four plain-clothes gendarmes had kept the beach under constant surveillance since the day of the murder. They kept a low profile, noting each day the behaviour of people strolling past the crime scene. That day, their patience was rewarded.

In the early afternoon, I received a call from the unit supervisor.

'We're intrigued by the behaviour of a man in his forties,' he began. 'He's wearing a beige raincoat. He's not very tall and has a limp in his left leg. He keeps walking up and down the beach, looking for marks on the rocks. He's an odd customer. We're tailing him.'

I quickly joined the team. The suspect had just gone back to a van parked behind one of the apartment blocks overlooking the beach. I decided to bring him in. A few moments later, we began a search of his makeshift home. I could feel the team was on its toes. Perhaps he was our man ...

We rapidly searched the van, dismantled part of the bodywork and carefully examined all the knives found in the few bits of furniture it contained. Meanwhile, the man watched closely. His name was Gérard and he didn't seem bothered at all. I even had the feeling that he was admiring our professionalism with the appreciation of a connoisseur. We took him into the local gendarmerie. The interview began.

'Have you been living in that van long?'

'Ever since my divorce. I started drinking. A friend gave me his van last November. I don't do much with my time. I get up quite late, around noon. I cook – mainly canned food ... In the afternoon, I hang around the van. I don't see many people. From time to time, a neighbour, Martin, comes to see me and we have a glass of red. He's the one who told me about the murder.'

'What were you doing that day?

'In the early afternoon, I was having a snooze on the bed in my van. Then Martin came and knocked at the door, after whistling from his window. He told me that a woman had just had her throat slit on the beach. I didn't go and have a look straight away, I waited till the next day. I don't like crowds. The police were still at the scene. From what I read in *Le Télégramme* and *Ouest-France*, the victim's name was Aline Pérès. I saw her photo. I might have met her during my stays at the Hôpital Morvan, but I'm not sure. According to the papers, her bag was found nearby and she hadn't been raped. I'd like to have seen the body to see how it was done. I say that because I was in the police for a while, that's the only reason, you understand.'

I was intrigued by this character and disturbed by his interest in the details of the murder. I pursued my line of questioning. 'Could you describe the victim?'

'Again, only from what I've read. She was forty-nine, divorced, mid-length brown hair.'

This behaviour foxed us. Was he speaking the truth, or was it a serious lead? It was vital to establish his movements on 14 May. His neighbour, Martin, was also brought in for questioning, and then his friends were interviewed, and their apartments and cars searched. In the end, we had nothing on him. Another red herring. Once again, time and energy had been spent only to conclude that here was a character who was definitely bizarre, but nothing more.

On 19 June at 10.30 a.m., the gendarmerie at Saint-Clair-sur-l'Elle in the Manche region received a call. One of the homeless men from the Emmaüs hostel whom we'd been looking for had

just been picked up. I left Brest at once. The longest a person can be held without charge is forty-eight hours from the time they are stopped, and the countdown had begun. There wasn't a second to lose. After the forty-eight hours have elapsed, the suspect cannot be rearrested. I stopped off at the Rennes gendarmerie en route. I needed backup, for this type of interview was likely to take time. Major 'JR' – his initials had become his nickname – was on duty. He was a good investigator, one of the pillars of the force. It was a real stroke of luck that he was there. He came with me.

3 p.m., Saint-Clair-sur-l'Elle, at last, after hours on the winding rural roads of Lower Normandy. At the gendarmerie, one of the chiefs greeted us.

'Your client is here, in the next office,' he said. 'He's a strange character. He's waiting for you. We've looked in his bag, there's nothing suspicious. You'll see for yourself. He told us he was caught travelling on a train without a ticket. He claims that's why he was hitch-hiking through here. He doesn't know why he's being held.'

I appreciated his professionalism. Nobody had mentioned the murder and that was just as well. The door to the office was ajar, and I observed the man unseen by him. He was standing waiting. I knew almost nothing about him. No previous convictions, no fixed abode. He was there simply because he'd been staying in the Emmaüs hostel at Le Relecq-Kerhuon on the eve of the murder.

As I watched him, I tried to get his measure. The first contact in custody is often difficult, yet I hoped I could break the ice quickly. If I couldn't get through to him, or if he took against me, then JR would take over. I glimpsed him in profile, standing in a corner of the room with his hands behind his back. He was tall, about one metre ninety, and thin, with short, straight brown hair. I knew he was thirty, but it was hard to tell his age. He wasn't unkempt, but was poorly dressed in a blue, yellow and red-striped short-sleeved shirt and blue canvas trousers. He held himself erect and seemed tense and jumpy, with an anxious expression. He kept jerking his head to examine the office windows one by one. He reminded me of a caged animal.

Major JR was ready, and we walked in. The man spun round. His alert brown eyes bored into me. His face was contorted by a grimace, as if some inner pain was eating him. What an expression! I tried not to show any surprise and walked towards him with a pleasant 'Good afternoon!' Then there was a brief, limp handshake. He shunned physical contact. He did not take his eyes off me. Suddenly I realised I was the only officer in plain clothes. JR too proffered his hand.

I decided to take the initiative before things became uncomfortable. In a reassuring voice, I said, 'I'm sorry to detain you but we need to speak to you, to ask you a few questions about your movements. It shouldn't take long. We're just setting up the typewriter and then we'll start. Can I get you anything?'

He was still staring at me. His lips were pinched and I noticed his fists were clenched.

'Are you from Saint-Lô?'

I realised then that he thought I came from the neighbouring town. As I wasn't in uniform, he assumed I outranked the others. I smiled at him, as if acquiescing.

'Would you please state your name.'

'My name is Francis Heaulme,' he began flatly. 'I was born on 25 February 1959 in Metz.'

'You're older than me, but only a few days.'

'So I could even call you by your first name,' he grinned back.

I agreed, it sometimes makes things easier. Sitting in front of the typewriter, I foresaw a tricky interview. He went on, in a controlled tone, 'I'm currently out of work and I stay at various Emmaüs hostels ...'

To avoid asking questions about the murder too soon, I then said, 'Francis, could you tell me about yourself? How did you end up on the road?'

He replied naturally, almost relieved, 'I grew up in my parents' home. I have a twenty-two-year-old sister. My mother died in 1984. My father remarried. I did all my studies in Metz. At seventeen, I qualified as an industrial electrician at the Fabert technical college. At eighteen, I signed up for two years in the territorial army. I served in radio communications in Frankfurt. In those days, I took part in manoeuvres. Although I was in the radio section, I did combat training. They taught different fighting techniques, and I learnt how to use a knife.'

My fingers poised on the keyboard, I held my breath. What an opening! What was he leading up to? His intense gaze still drilled into mine. He spoke in fits and starts, interspersed with endless pauses. He was in control of himself. Was he testing us out? Heaulme was disconcerting. I knew I must show no emotion, no reaction.

He went on, 'For example, to take out a guard you have to surprise him from behind. You use your left hand to raise his head and make sure you place your forearm over his mouth to stop him shouting. With your right hand you stab him in the carotid, then in the heart, and one last time in the spine. In any case, you have to use all your strength ... I even saw films about these things in the army.'

I did not answer. I discreetly tried to catch JR's eye. I found it hard to believe what I had just heard. The major did not react. And yet Francis Heaulme had just described the way in which Aline Pérès had been killed. Was it provocation, a coincidence? It wasn't possible, the investigation was over, it had to be him ...

The interview continued:

'After the army, I worked as an electrician for my father, and then for two or three contractors. In 1984, my mother died. I took it very badly and tried to kill myself with a shotgun. I can't remember the date, but my mother died on a Sunday evening, and I tried to kill myself three days later. After that I was sent to a psychiatric hospital in Jury-lès-Metz. I was sectioned by the Prefect. When I came out, I started working again. After that incident, I was on medication, I was given anti-anxiety pills. In January 1988, when I was living at 12, Rue Charlemagne in Metz, I packed my bag on impulse and got on a train to Nice. I didn't know where I was going. Since then, I've stayed at different Emmaüs communities in France.'

I gently interrupted him and asked him to talk to me about the previous month, i.e. May.

'I have to tell you that I spent most of May 1989 at the Emmaüs community in Brest. I arrived there at the end of April and I left the day before a woman was killed on the beach near the hostel. I left on a Saturday evening, after asking the director, Mr Pascal, for my wages, 520 francs.'

I didn't know what to think. He referred directly to the crime and went into detail. I remained impassive.

'I caught a bus near the Longchamp bar, six hundred metres from the hostel,' he continued. 'That bus took me directly to Guilers, to my friend Raymond's house. I had met him at the Emmaüs auction room in Brest. I'd never been to his house, but he'd given me his address. I've lost it since. I spent the night in Guilers and on the Sunday I took the train from Brest to Saint-Brieuc at around eight or nine o'clock.'

That meant he had left the community but remained in the area. I wondered who this man was. He was still staring at me fixedly. It was extraordinary, he did not blink. I felt he was on the verge of exploding.

He rattled off his journey without difficulty. 'I stayed in Saint-Brieuc for two days and then I went down to Quimperlé. That's where I stayed in the psychiatric hospital.'

I wanted to ask him why, but I allowed him to follow his train of thought.

'I sort of ran away from the psychiatric hospital in Quimperlé. From there I took the train back to Saint-Brieuc where I slept for two days at the Emmaüs hostel. Then I hitched to San Malo and Cherbourg. In one day. In fact I arrived in Cherbourg on 22 June and stayed there until Wednesday 28 at the Emmaüs hostel. On 28 June, I took the train to Caen. But I got off too soon because I was drunk …'

He was constantly on the move. He had a good memory for dates and places, unlike most of the vagrants I had met recently.

'I should tell you that I often drink. I take anti-anxiety pills, and other medication. It's bad for me to drink, because it gives me urges. I fantasise about fight scenes with a knife, I see my hands covered in blood. I feel the need to look at my hands to see if it's true.'

What an astonishing confession! I was convinced that I was sitting opposite Aline Pérès's killer. It was almost too easy, all I had to do was listen. I shot Major JR another look. I felt he was on the same wavelength. He signalled to me to allow Heaulme to continue. Francis Heaulme watched our reaction.

'In the past,' he went on, 'I don't know exactly when, probably in 1988, when I was in Dijon, I even acted out my fantasy. For no reason, I felt this urge and I attacked a woman. In the middle of a pedestrian street, I grabbed a woman by the arms and squeezed very hard. She screamed and I let go. I hid and nobody caught me. I went to see a doctor to tell him about my problem. I was never charged, even though a police inspector questioned me.'

I let him speak and asked him to go back to his stay in Brest.

'On 10 May 1989,' replied Heaulme, 'I went with Henri L from the Emmaüs community to the beach where the murder took place on 14 May. I suddenly felt an urge. I wanted to attack a girl. She was aged about eighteen or twenty. She was coming out of the water. She was wearing a bikini. I ran towards her to grab her. I wasn't armed, I had nothing in my hand. But in my pocket I did have a knife with a wooden handle. The girl began to scream and ran towards a man who was her father. This man grabbed my arm and called me names. That brought me to my senses. A few moments later, I felt ill and Henri L went to get somebody from the Emmaüs community to help me back there. In the community, a doctor came to examine me. After receiving treatment, I carried on with my usual activities. But then, on the Thursday evening, I felt the urge to go back to the beach again to do something. So I went down at around 8 p.m., after supper. I didn't have a knife, only a piece of cable that I could use as a cosh. I didn't do anything that day.'

What was all this about and who was this individual? It was 6.30 p.m., we had already been listening to Heaulme for three hours. I urgently needed to talk with my colleague. We broke off the interview, but decided to keep him in custody. We had to find a hotel. I thought we would need forty-eight hours, perhaps less. We had to find a strategy. I was convinced he was the murderer. We couldn't let him go without telling us more. I had heard too much, or not enough.

In the car I asked Major JR what his thoughts were. His reply alarmed me.

'I have already come across this type who rambles on and sometimes strikes close to the truth. Besides, if he were really the killer, he would never have talked to us like that.'

In a second, he had turned Heaulme's attitude on its head, making his declarations sound like the best possible defence.

'He's bound to have read the papers and he's stringing us along.'

I reminded him of the victim's wounds and what our suspect claimed to have learnt in the army.

'He opened up like that because he thinks I'm from Saint-Lô, not from Brest. He thinks I won't make the connection with the Moulin Blanc affair. He's manipulative.'

It was no use. The major would not back down. A wise reaction or appalling blindness? In spite of everything, I had high hopes that the rest of the interview would prove me right.

8.30 p.m. After having eaten dinner and given Francis Heaulme a sandwich, we resumed. I asked him what he had been planning to do on the beach that Thursday evening with a cosh.

'When I mentioned Thursday evening to you,' Francis replied, 'I should tell you that I was planning to break into a car. In the end, I didn't do anything and I went back to the hostel at around 10 p.m.'

The atmosphere had changed. Heaulme was aware that he was in danger. He suspected he had said too much. He had probably realised that I was not an investigator from Saint-Lô.

'I didn't go to the beach on Friday 12 May, but I did go there on the 13th, after work. I was with Henri L, at around 8 p.m. Henri shared my room at the hostel. He is about forty years old. He wears a black leather bomber jacket and has short, greying hair. It was definitely that day, 13 May, that after supper I decided to leave. It was 8 p.m. when I asked for my wages. I had no particular reason for leaving, it was a spur-of-the-moment decision. That evening I was wearing black trousers and a white shirt, and I was carrying my rucksack.'

'What about Sunday 14 May?'

'I recall going to sleep on the beach at Brest, opposite the bus stop near the bar called the Longchamp.'

Suddenly, he stopped talking and changed his demeanour. He straightened up and looked at me as if he were emerging from a dream. 'I have to add to some of the things I've told you. First of all, on 13 May 1989, during the afternoon, I hitch-hiked to Quimper. Secondly, when I got to Quimper, I had a giddy spell and I was taken to hospital. I was sent to the cardiology ward of the Laënnec hospital. I stayed there until 16 May 1989, the day I moved into the community at Quimperlé. So I have no connection with your case.'

The thread had just snapped. I pressed him, 'Francis, are you certain about what you're saying?'

He clammed up. By now it was 11.30 p.m. I left the office and grabbed a telephone. It was vital to check his whereabouts on 14 May. I was sure that he had not been in Quimper hospital on the Sunday afternoon. I picked up the receiver and asked for the cardiology ward. I was asked to ring back the next day. I explained the urgency of the situation, and that I needed to check whether Francis Heaulme had indeed been an in-patient there on 14 May. The duty nurse checked the ward register.

'The gentleman in question was a patient here, in the cardiology ward, from 13 to 16 May 1989.'

It couldn't be true. That was eighty kilometres away from Moulin Blanc beach. I refused to believe it. I probed further. Had he left the ward on the Sunday afternoon? I added that I suspected that he had been involved in an assault. The nurse assured me that you can't just walk out of a cardiology ward and return a few hours later. I was politely informed that people didn't just wander in and out. Then I called the Quimper gendarmerie to ask to have a team sent straight to the hospital to check the records. I waited. My colleagues would probably discover the source of the error.

Meanwhile, Francis Heaulme was in the adjoining room. Half-past midnight. The telephone rang. The chief of the Quimper gendarmerie on the line assured me that they had checked everything, and that our suspect had not gone out that day. Something wasn't right, and I still wouldn't believe it. In the meantime, the presumed killer had an alibi, and I couldn't hold him any longer. I returned to the office and discreetly told Major JR the results of my inquiries. He didn't seem particularly surprised. He was even condescending. In his eyes, I could read: 'Young and inexperienced, getting all worked up over nothing ...'

Even so, I wondered whether it wouldn't be better to keep Heaulme in custody while we confiscated his hospital record. I called the investigating magistrate and explained the situation. He thought it better to let him go so as not to use up the last hours of custody. I volunteered to go to the cardiology ward myself, the next day.

I went back to the office. Heaulme was amused, relaxed. He

knew that we had nothing on him. As it was getting late, he asked me if he could sleep there, in a cell. Why not? I had no reason to say no.

'I'll wake you up at 7 o'clock.'

'Thanks to you, I had a good night,' he said, without any shame and without the slightest hint of irony.

Before he left, we had a coffee together. I tried to understand this strange character a little better, but he didn't speak. I ventured to say to him, 'If you have a problem, if you start seeing war scenes again, don't be afraid to seek medical help.'

He retorted, 'François, you'd make a good psychiatrist!'

François instead of Jean-François — had he registered my first name or not? I made a mental note but said nothing.

Some mug shots were taken. Amused, he gave me his identity photo. I took a sample of mud from the soles of his shoes. A search of his rucksack yielded nothing and the clothes he owned came from charity, the Secours Catholique in Caen. He had no knife, no letters. I did not glean any more clues.

Finally, we parted company. I watched him set off calmly in the direction of Caen, with his shambling gait and his rucksack slung over his shoulder. I had the feeling that something serious was happening but that I couldn't do anything about it.

I made my way back to Rennes, with a heavy heart, while as far as Major JR was concerned, Heaulme was off the hook. I felt disappointed, and was still wondering what had really happened.

Four hours later, I was in Quimper. I went straight to the cardiology ward and asked to see the senior cardiologist. He appeared at the end of a long corridor, accompanied by two nurses. The doctor had already been informed of my investigation. He was holding Francis Heaulme's medical records. I told him of my serious doubts about Heaulme's presence on 14 May. He listened to me politely, and brought out a temperature chart that put an end to our conversation. There was an entry: 'Francis Heaulme, 14 May 1989, 5 p.m.' It stated that the patient had no temperature at 5 p.m., the time of the murder. The alibi was rock-solid. How on earth could it be possible?

The only thing left for me to do was to find Henri L with whom Francis Heaulme had spent his time before the murder. A few hours of inquiries in the Brest area, and my suspicions had been confirmed.

3

On the trail of
the killer

Back at the gendarmerie in Le Relecq-Kerhuon, I wanted a full
report on my desk as soon as possible so that an analysis of the
findings so far could be handed over to the investigators. My
two colleagues, Jean-Claude and Jean-Paul, had listened attentively to my account of my interview with Francis Heaulme.
They warned me that this case risked damaging the unit's repu-
tation, it seemed such a cock-eyed line of inquiry. We decided
to organise a meeting with all the teams of investigators.

That day, there were some new faces among the familiar
ones. All the top brass from Brest central police station had
turned out – a sign that things were going to be difficult. In a
tense atmosphere, the discussion began.

Jean-Claude and Jean-Paul went over the different areas of

Aline Pérès's life, point by point. Their method of working reminded me of the slow advance of a steamroller: they sifted through her work life, family, acquaintances and love life. One by one, they cited the witnesses who had been close to the victim and listed those still to be followed up.

The further their statement went, the less convinced I was that this was the right way to go. The answer lay elsewhere. Aline Pérès had led a quiet life. This murder had no apparent motive. Had it been a gratuitous act or that of a maniac? Or was it premeditated? Impossible not to go over it again … In my head I could still hear Francis Heaulme's blank, monotonous voice … That stilted voice forming the words one by one, counting them out like something precious, and then suddenly falling silent. Words interspersed with strange silences heightened by an intense, fixed gaze.

I could not accept that all the things he had told me were mere coincidence. And the same question kept rearing its head, all the more insistently as I felt more and more that I was the only person seeking the answer. Who was Francis Heaulme? Who was this odd character?

It was the turn of Bertrand's team to speak. They were still looking for new witnesses in Le Relecq-Kerhuon. Tireless in their efforts, they had managed to find some others. The local weather forecast of 14 May helped establish the time that visitors had started arriving on the beach, for on that day it had not turned really sunny until 3 p.m. Thus, one by one, the pieces of the jigsaw began to fit together. Each individual could be situated in relation to the others, against this background surrounding the scene of the crime. A few grey areas still remained. One in particular: who was the man that several witnesses had seen sitting on the rocks above the victim? The investigations had also confirmed that residents from the Emmaüs communities did hang around the beach, but we had too little information to identify them. The fact was, we barely knew who they were.

François, the boss of the investigation brigade, went on with his report. The leads had all gone cold. The local delinquents had nothing to say on the matter. The ex-convicts released before the attack had been tracked down, and rumours of all sorts that had been going round the town had been refuted. When we reached the case of the Brest castle attacker on the evening of 14 May, who was still at large, my colleagues' expressions made it clear that many of them thought he was our man.

Then it was my turn. I could tell that some people were just waiting for me to slip up so that they could take me off the case. A few minutes were enough to summarise my meeting with Francis Heaulme, which had been surprising to say the least. I went over every detail. I had barely finished before the reactions began. Those who knew me shot me questioning looks. They hoped that I had judged the situation accurately. Others were sceptical and said so. But still I insisted: we had to draw up a proper work plan. Retrace every step of the suspect's movements in Brest, of course, but also track down other regulars from the beach, identify new vagrants and locate the men who had been staying at the Emmaüs community on 14 May. I concluded by informing them of my decision to return to Quimper hospital. There was certainly one detail that had escaped me. The atmosphere was downright hostile.

The meeting over, I was summoned by the company commander of the Brest gendarmerie, who was highly critical of my leadership of the investigation.

'I don't understand why you don't involve all the investigators in finding the Brest castle attacker. There's no doubt he's the murderer!'

His tone was brittle. This was a man with a short fuse. I pointed out to him that the suspect in question was being sought by the city's police force and that the victim had lodged a complaint. I added, 'It is a related incident, which is being taken into consideration. There's a team of investigators on the case. Furthermore, we have an interesting lead with Francis Heaulme.'

'You call that a lead!? I think we'd better work separately!'

Clearly annoyed, he concluded the conversation with, 'From today, the number of men at your disposal will be cut to the minimum!'

Lack of understanding of the workings of an investigation, defence of his patch, or professional jealousy? To this day, I find it hard to understand the real reasons behind his decision. In any case, it was final. From the next day, at the Relecq-Kerhuon gendarmerie, the number of men melted like snow in the sun.

Fortunately, my status of investigator allowed me to bypass the hierarchy. The number of men had been cut, but the main teams were still in place. We would pursue our investigations with or without the help of our colleagues in Brest.

We now had a photograph of Francis Heaulme which was

routinely shown to the witnesses interviewed. Bertrand then informed me that there had never been a Henri L at the Emmaüs community. I also learned that our suspect had been declared unfit for service and that he had never been in the army. Furthermore, the nature of the blows to the victim had not appeared in the press. That was a start. But Heaulme's hospital alibi still stood up.

I returned as planned to the Laënnec hospital in Quimper. After several days, although the ice had not been completely broken, my relations with the staff had thawed a little. They were cagey at first, but gradually they opened up, eventually disclosing a few little secrets. The arrival of Francis Heaulme on 13 May 1989 had not gone unnoticed. Brought into casualty on the Saturday evening by the fire brigade, after he had passed out on the public highway, he was admitted to the cardiology ward.

'The fact is, he needed rest, not treatment ... In other words, there was nothing wrong with his heart. He'd had a bit to drink ... I remember, we put him in Mr K's room,' a nurse told me.

This patient, a retired teacher, was still in hospital. Would he remember the man in the next bed? Might he have noticed anything?

I visited him in his room. The sixty-five-year-old man lying on his bed looked frail, but he greeted me with a smile. Inevitably, I was reminded of the school teacher he had been. I pictured him calm and attentive towards his students.

'Good afternoon, Mr K,' I said. 'I'm Chief Abgrall from the Rennes gendarmerie. I hope I'm not disturbing you.'

He replied with a smile, 'Not at all. Do come in!'

His voice was warm and assured. This interview was going to be helpful.

'My job is to check the movements of a particular person on 14 May last. A long weekend. Do you remember?'

'I think so. I'll do my best to recollect ... What do you want to know?'

I asked him to look at the identity photo that Francis Heaulme had given me while I set up my typewriter.

'I remember this man,' he declared, pointing at the photo. 'He shared my room. He was tall. He only stayed here the weekend of 13 to 15 May. He told me he came from Lorraine and he talked about the Emmaüs communities.'

'Do you remember if this man stayed here in the room all the time, or whether he went out for a while?'

'I think he stayed here,' he went on after a moment's thought, 'but I'm not certain. I think that if he did go out, it wasn't for long. He spent his time sleeping, or reading the magazines I lent him. On reflection, I remember discussing his departure with one of the nurses, because she'd found sand under his bed. Then we talked about the murder committed in Brest that weekend.'

The man weighed his words, as if sensing the importance of his evidence.

'If you talked about the murder, it was because he'd been out, wasn't it?'

'As I told you, as far as I remember, if he went out, it was only for a short while!' he rapped.

His reply was categorical, but he couldn't remember which

nurse he'd had the conversation with. So he was not in a position to give an accurate appraisal of the length of time his room mate had been away. Once again, it struck me that the key to this case was in the unspoken, the hints and silences.

Pursuing our conversation, I then asked him about the routine for checking the patients' temperatures. Without showing any surprise at my question, he provided an answer which was a vital key:

'At the weekend it's different from weekdays ... Our temperatures are taken at around 4 to 4.30 p.m. by the nurses. They write down the temperature shown on the thermometer placed on the bedside table ...'

Placed on the bedside table! ... Which implied that the patients were not always present when their temperature was noted. At that point, I saw a glimmer of hope. I went on, 'If someone is away from their bed when the nurses come by, what do they do?'

'The thermometer is placed on the bedside table at around 1 p.m.,' he explained. 'If the patient isn't there when they come round, they write down the temperature shown, even if the patient isn't present.'

That was it! If this information were confirmed by a nurse, Francis Heaulme's temperature chart could no longer be considered a definite alibi. I immediately asked to see the nurses' rota for 14 May. Unfortunately, each interview proved fruitless. None of them remembered, or wanted to remember, the 14th of May. There was a certain unease, and no wonder ...

A nurse told me, 'You won't find anyone who'll admit that a

temperature was taken in the patient's absence. It's enough to lose you your job ... The doctors take that very seriously. But, I can tell you, it does happen ... Especially in cases like yours, the patient who wasn't really ill. It was a kind of respite care for him ... On the other hand, I can assure you the rooms are cleaned every day. There's no way sand would stay under the bed for more than a day.'

That was a big step forward. The truth seemed within my grasp, but it was still elusive.

In Brest, the investigating magistrate had been following the progress of the inquiry step by step since the first hour. On my return from Quimper, we met for lunch. We are the same age. He is from Brest and was surprised at the unusual nature of this murder. In a little restaurant in town, over salad and a bottle of mineral water, I told him my feelings about this case.

I kept nothing from him. The man was attentive, one of the only people, so far, who seemed to give some credence to my investigations. I felt a measure of relief. However, he was adamant: there were no grounds for arresting the vagrant who had been admitted to hospital as a casualty.

It was already August. Two months had gone by since Aline Pérès's murder, and we had got nowhere, or next to nowhere. The days went by, and no further important information had come in. 'We must widen the search and go straight to the source ...' Jop, my former partner would often say ...

Within the gendarmerie, people often say, 'listen to the voice of experience.' I took this motto to heart and went off to install myself at number 1, Boulevard Théophile-Sueur in Rosny-sous-Bois, in Seine-Saint-Denis, just outside Paris. This is the home of the gendarmerie's forensic research centre and archives. I knew no better source of information. All the crimes and offences committed in France are recorded and archived here, and requests for information on individuals all pass through this office. Perhaps I might find records of a case resembling the murder on the beach, with similarities or parallels that the computer check had not identified.

Serge L, one of the heads of department, was used to seeing me come in and go through the archives with a fine-tooth comb; this wasn't the first time that I had made this move in an investigation. He greeted me with a smile and said cheerfully, 'Your office is ready!'

Having expressed our pleasure at meeting again, we quickly went to the heart of the subject. I had barely finished when he brought me a telex.

'Look what I've just received,' he said. 'It's a request for information from the Avignon gendarmerie concerning an individual called Francis Heaulme. There's been an unusual murder in the area.'

This time, luck was on my side.

Two phone calls and a few hundred kilometres later, I was in the Vaucluse region, heading towards Courthézon accompanied by the chief of the Avignon gendarmerie, who had offered to drive me there. His case was indeed odd: the body of a sixty-year-old man had been found in the undergrowth beside a river lying by a footpath that led to an Emmaüs community. His skull had been battered with a rock.

Emmaüs ... an extraordinary coincidence ...

The car pulled up. We set off on foot down a shrub-fringed path running through a coppice to the banks of the Ouvèze. Soon we caught sight of the parched river bed.

'The body was discovered over there, under that tree. He was killed on the shingle. The victim had no trousers on. But we did find a pair of jeans ten metres away. They would fit a very tall person and were bloodstained. In a pocket was a scrap of paper with only six figures of a phone number on it ... You can see the brutality of the attack from the photos. I don't understand what happened.'

The body had already been lying there for twenty-four hours when it was discovered. The man, formerly in the Foreign Legion, had been living in the area for years. He was single and led a quiet life.

The crime scene reminded me of Moulin Blanc beach. A man attacked beside water, a road nearby, an Emmaüs community not far away, and the extraordinary violence of the attack.

And then, while we were driving, the chief came out with a significant piece of information:

'You know, Courthézon is near the place where the man called Francis Heaulme was stopped. The day the body was discovered, he was wearing a pair of Bermudas.'

There was one major difference however: the victim was a man.

At the Avignon gendarmerie, I told my colleagues about the investigation being conducted in Brest. The chief reckoned the similarity between the two cases was interesting, but he added, 'Heaulme had just come from Marseille, where he'd been in hospital. So he's in the clear this time. That means I've got nothing to ask him.'

'Yes, but each time he's supposed to be in hospital, somebody dies in the vicinity of an Emmaüs community ... In any case, you could always ask him to try on the jeans found near the victim!'

My last argument struck a chord. The chief decided to add Heaulme's name to the wanted list. He promised to let me know as soon as he'd been located. We parted company on these words.

Before returning to Brittany, I had to carry out two final checks. Stepping through the porch of the Emmaüs community in Bédarrides, I saw, across the courtyard, a single-storey building bathed in light, with all the windows open wide. It was a welcoming place. Heaulme was not on the register. 'We usually write down the names of all the visitors in the register. Occasionally we forget, for someone who only stays one night,' explained the director.

At the Marseille-Nord hospital, Francis Heaulme had not been seen since the morning of Saturday 7 August. Precisely the date when the retired legionnaire had been murdered.

Meanwhile, the investigation in Brest had made some headway. Evidence of Francis Heaulme's presence had been found. The captain of the army recruitment centre had seen all sorts wanting to enlist, but he had been particularly struck by our suspect's application.

'It was back in May, around the 15th ...'

'He kept insisting, telling me he lived in a hostel, that he was hard up and that the army was his only way out ... He told me he wanted to kill. After a pause, he added: "For France." It was that afterthought that struck me ... What really shocked me was his eagerness to kill.'

Once again, clues, odd coincidences, but no proof.

The months went by, and Francis Heaulme was still at large somewhere in France. The summer was over, and winter was already in the air. I felt as though I was wasting time and the investigation was stagnating.

It was 1 p.m. on Sunday 19 November when I received a call from the chief of the Avignon gendarmerie. 'Francis Heaulme has just been stopped in Meurthe-et-Moselle. He's being held at the gendarmerie in Blainville-sur-l'Eau. I'm getting the first train out. I'll meet you there.'

A call to the officer on duty in the criminal investigation unit and I was on the road again. It was raining buckets and the weather was cold. The journey seemed endless.

10 p.m. It had been dark for hours when I finally reached the gendarmerie. The chief had just arrived, and was visibly exhausted from the long train journey. He hadn't yet seen Francis Heaulme, who was being kept in another room. We briefly

filled each other in on the progress of our respective investigations. Nothing new. I ventured one last warning. 'Above all, don't go by his physical appearance, he takes advantage of it. Don't underestimate him, he's manipulative.'

Although my colleague didn't seem on good form, he was convinced he could get the better of Heaulme.

'I have some incriminating evidence,' he retorted.

On his way to the interview room, Heaulme walked past me escorted by a gendarme. He hadn't changed. His eyes betrayed his surprise at seeing me there. He called out, 'Hello, François!' He remembered me all right, still calling me by the wrong name. I proffered my hand. His limp handshake took me right back to Normandy …

It was going to be a long tough interview. The chief announced point-blank that he was investigating a homicide and that Heaulme was in the frame. Francis Heaulme declared he knew nothing about it before describing his journey from Marseille to Orange, from Courthézon to Bédarrides. He went into masses of detail … Stories that could not be corroborated, I was convinced.

Heaulme was ice-cool. At 1.30 a.m., the interview was over. The chief was visibly irritated and told me he was wasting his time. He left the gendarmerie at once. The next day, there was to be a search of the room Francis Heaulme had slept in at the Emmaüs community in Mont-sur-Meurthe. Meanwhile he was to spend the night at the gendarmerie. I took my chance and walked him back to his cell, starting up a conversation.

'Well, Francis, you often end up in custody. When I heard

you were here, I thought I should come and see you.'

Francis turned his head towards me but did not reply. He was pensive, tired. He put his belongings down on a little table – a few coins, an old lighter – and then removed his shoe laces. On entering the secure cell, he turned towards me. We were standing very close, and I had to look up to see his face. Calmly, he replied, 'François, I know you know ... this business was a bit of a cock-up.'

A confession in disguise? Francis Heaulme in all his ambiguity. I tried to cover up my surprise.

'I'm listening, Francis, that's what I'm here for.'

'Leave me alone. I know you know, but it's all "The Gaul's" fault. That's all, now I'm going to sleep.'

His tone had changed. Heaulme had recovered his composure. He was back in his own world again. It was worse than I had thought. He had almost been within my grasp but he had slipped through my fingers. My hunch was that the Moulin Blanc killing was not his only murder, but once again I couldn't nail him.

The next day, at 11 a.m., the chief had finished his checks. My conversation with Francis did not convince him. His mind was now made up.

'He was in Marseille-Nord hospital, wasn't he?'

Three-quarters of an hour later, when Heaulme was released, I tried one last tactic.

'Francis, are you sure you haven't got something you want to tell me?'

'No!' he replied obstinately.

'Who's "The Gaul"?'

'He's a Gaul, that's all!'

He didn't want to talk any more, and asked me to leave him alone. I walked with him to the gate. Powerless, I watched him leave for the second time. I felt isolated and above all concerned. Nobody seemed to realise that Heaulme's beanpole physique, which was not much to look at, could be concealing a highly dangerous murderer. Had we let a vicious killer get away with murder?

4

'The Gaul'

January 1990. Time was going by and the Moulin Blanc murderer was still at large ... As was the Brest castle attacker. In the latter case, the police investigation was following the line that it was just a gangland incident – as a matter of fact, the victim was now behind bars.

As for my investigation, my staff had been squeezed even further. Jean-Claude and Jean-Paul had gone off to work on other cases. They had left me their charts of Aline's life. An entire existence mapped out on paper, in the tiniest detail, but nothing that shed any light on why she had been murdered. Meanwhile, Bertrand had gone back to his local unit at Le Relecq-Kerhuon. In Brest, thanks to my boss's extremely diplomatic intervention, the differences of opinion had softened somewhat. The criminal investigation unit agreed to share information that might be of interest to us. Time would tell. Meanwhile, I no longer had a permanent partner. The original team had been pared down to the bone. Anyone would think that Aline Pérès's death no longer mattered.

These lengthy investigations are rarely welcomed by the various department heads. They balk at staffing an incident room for more than a few weeks. Those who are working on a murder case do nothing else. When it drags on, as it often does given the extensive investigations involved, the case is soon seen as a waste of time and money. Dramatic reductions in resources are quite often preceded by sometimes futile arrests. A way of justifying themselves before the magistrates: if the culprit hasn't been nailed, it's not for want of trying.

But a few investigators continue to keep their ear to the ground and will come and lend a hand at any point.

Meanwhile, I pursued the investigation. The homeless had become my priority, with 'The Gaul' as my chief target. Francis Heaulme had deliberately mentioned his name. He was surely one of the keys to the puzzle. Most of the drifters who hung around the Moulin Blanc beach had been identified and located. Since the murder, they had scattered all over France. Some were in Saint-Brieuc on the Côtes-d'Armor in Brittany, others at Douai in the north, in Lyon, Bordeaux or Paris. One by one, I went and interviewed them. A venture that required a lot of patience, for they are always on the move, and I sometimes had to approach them in unorthodox ways. In once instance, in the 13th arrondissement in Paris, I had to masquerade as a benefits office clerk. There was no photograph of this witness. We only knew his name and the district where he was supposedly living.

I had to wait several days until he came to collect his benefits and I could finally interview him.

The twenty or so vagrants interviewed and the thousands of kilometres covered yielded very little useful information. Nothing, in any case, that would lead me to 'The Gaul', who seemed to have disappeared into thin air. Nothing about Heaulme or his stay at the Emmaüs community either, or about the beach on the day of the murder. But I was not overly worried. From experience, I knew that clues could come to light even a long time after the event.

Paris, Monday 13 June 1990, 12.45 p.m. Didier M was stopped by a police patrol at the Austerlitz railway station. This man was the former cook at the Emmaüs community in Le Relecq-Kerhuon. He had been there over a year ago, that fatal Sunday 14 May 1989. Luckily my former colleague Jean-Claude was working in Paris. I asked him to hold the fort until I could get there. He and a colleague took charge of this witness.

Meanwhile, I grabbed the photo album from the file, which had a list of all the witnesses interviewed since the beginning of the investigation, and set off for the capital. I got caught in the traffic jams just outside Paris, and it was after 9 p.m. when I reached the gendarmerie in the Rue des Minimes. More than three hours wasted ...

The minute I arrived, Jean-Claude came out to greet me.

'He's been told he's being held for questioning,' he informed me, 'and we've started going through his history. He's relaxed, but not very talkative. We haven't mentioned the murder.'

'What does he look like?'

'Age thirty-five. Born in northern France. Fair hair, average height, solid. He's been homeless for about ten years. We found a knife in his belongings. He says he's had it since the army. In any case, this knife can't be the one used by the killer. It's a chrome and nickel alloy ... There, he's all yours. He's expecting you.'

When I walked into the office where we were going to be interviewing him, Didier M was in a truculent mood. He had been returning from the funeral of his twin brother when he'd been stopped. He did not understand why he was being kept in custody, especially under the circumstances ... He had the blank, hard face of a man who'd not been dealt many favours. His story reminded me of that of the many drifters I'd met those last few weeks. Family hard up, failure at school, petty crime, spells in jail ... But that didn't make Didier M a criminal. He had left his turbulent past behind him long ago.

He moved from community to community, working as a cook. That gave him board and lodging, and at the end of the month a small wage of barely 500 francs [£50]. That day, he had 200 francs in his pocket. His entire fortune.

The introductions over, I began the interview with the usual general questions so as not to upset the witness from the outset. We began by retracing his road journey before his arrival in Brest in spring 1989. Boulogne-sur-Mer, Lens, Châteauroux, Bordeaux, Brest and Le Relecq-Kerhuon.

'You know, when you're homeless,' he explained as if by way of an excuse, 'it's impossible to settle in one place. Hostels only allow you to stay for a few days and you have to move on.'

'Can you tell us about any significant events that occurred during your stay in the community of Le Relecq-Kerhuon?' asked Jean-Claude.

'Yes,' he replied animatedly. 'One evening, a new arrival stole something from another resident. When he was found out, he ran away without waiting for the director. I saw him again at Saint-Brieuc. I don't know his name, but I could recognise him. He's tall, thin, has dark brown hair and wears glasses. He looks about forty. The other cook and I thought that there was something wrong with him, that he must be on medication or the bottle. He seemed to have memory problems.'

I showed him my album. 'Can you see him among these photographs? Take your time. Look at them all carefully.'

Didier M hadn't got to the end of the first page when he pointed at photo number 3. He was categorical, this was definitely the man who had committed the theft in the Emmaüs community. To our great surprise, Didier M had just identified Francis Heaulme. Our suspect had been careful not to disclose to me the precise reason for his departure ...

'Can you remember any other striking incidents that happened either inside or outside the community?'

'Yes, the murder on the beach. It was a Sunday ... Actually it was the day after the theft I just told you about ... That day almost the entire community was out.'

Hour by hour, Didier M pieced together that Sunday afternoon, detailing the various conversations and comings and goings of the residents. He spoke freely and tried to be as exact as possible. From having interviewed the other members of the community, I knew he was not lying. However, he did forget to mention where he was at 5 p.m., the time of the murder. Nothing about the following two hours either. This omission was suspect to say the least. What was he trying to hide?

I interrupted him.

'We know it's hard to remember what you were doing a year ago, but to build up the full picture of events, we need as many details as possible. Try to remember that particular weekend. Tell us what you did between Saturday 13 May and Monday 15 ...'

'I'll do my best, but it was a long time ago,' he continued wearily. 'On Saturday 13 May ... At 8 o'clock I served breakfast ... Around 1.30 I went for a stroll outside. I went and bought a bottle of rosé at the Super U and I sat on the rocks, under the trees, at the point that overlooks the beach. I liked going there. I often used to go and sit there. Around 3 o'clock, a former resident of the community, Philippe D, came up to me. He was a carpenter at the Emmaüs. We chatted and had a drink together. I thought he'd left the area and I was surprised that he was still around.'

So the day before the murder, these two men had been sitting in the very spot where, the next day, the killer would stake out his victim. Who was this Philippe D? I absolutely had to know more, but it was already 2.30 a.m. I could see that Didier M was getting tired of this question-and-answer session. I decided to suspend the interview. It wouldn't yield anything further.

While Didier M was being led to his cell, I couldn't resist making some inquiries. I sat down in front of the computer terminal. Confirmation of civil status, army record, convictions and prison sentences ... My high-priority requests were relayed to the central database. In a few hours, I would have my answers. Now it was time to get some rest.

9 a.m. An auxiliary gendarme handed me an envelope. Not very thick. It contained all the information that the central database had come up with on Philippe D, as well as a photograph. An old conviction for pick-pocketing was of little interest, but the photo of this man was so striking that I called Jean-Claude.

He had light brown hair cascading onto his shoulders, a long face with fine but well-defined features, and quite a large, bulbous nose. His eyes were light blue under shaggy eyebrows, and his lips were surrounded by a bushy, droopy moustache which gave him the distinct look of a warrior ... an ancient Gaul. I would bet my bottom dollar that Philippe D was Francis Heaulme's 'Gaul'!

Didier M's custody was extended. At 10 a.m. the interview resumed. He recognised Philippe D at once. There was no doubt about it, he was our man.

I picked up the thread from where we had left off. The day of 14 May, and, above all, what he was doing at the time of the murder. Didier M was visibly ill at ease. His answers were hesitant, awkward. Very quickly, he clammed up. He declared that he couldn't remember.

'All that was too long ago! Do you know what you were doing a year ago to the day, between 5 and 7 p.m.? How do you expect me to remember?' he concluded.

He had clearly been thinking during the few hours' rest he'd been granted. Once again, his behaviour intrigued me. What was he afraid of? Of no fixed abode, no wife, no friends, a knife in his bag ... and no alibi ... He had the profile of the ideal culprit. And yet, I couldn't see him as a murderer. Perhaps he was an accomplice? Or merely a witness?

That was the reasoning Didier M must have followed during the night. He was probably afraid of being accused. Better not say another word then. I decided to play a new card.

'I have in front of me the testimony of the director of the Emmaüs community who you spoke to a year ago,' I told him, showing him the name on the interview statement. 'He told us that on Monday 15, in other words the day after the murder, you talked to him at some length about the Moulin Blanc murder. You seemed perturbed. He even told us that you'd described a possible crime scenario. Is that true?'

Didier M was disconcerted. During the investigations I've carried out, I have often come across men like him. Rugged loners, often rejecting established social rules, but with their own particular code of honour to which they cling. His silence was proof of his solidarity with his travelling companions and fellow sufferers. Whatever they were. In his world, you never say anything compromising to the authorities ... but this time, the risk was too enormous, the affair too serious. Didier M eventually told us everything.

'On the Sunday, around 4.30 p.m., I went to meet Daniel, a mate of mine. He lives not far from the beach. He has a small apartment which he can afford with his benefits. We went for a drink together at the Longchamp. It's our regular café. We stayed there for a good hour or so. And then, suddenly, a fellow arrives saying there's a body on the beach. We ask him where. It's just by the spot where I like to hang out. That gives me the creeps. I don't want to go and have a look. There were too many people and the gendarmes were already there ...'

'Why didn't you tell me this earlier?'

'I didn't want to be fingered for the killing ... and anyway, it's none of my business.'

'But you did go back to the scene the next day, didn't you?'

'Yes, it's true, but simply out of curiosity, I swear I had the Monday off. After breakfast I went down to the Longchamp. There, I read about the murder in the paper. It was on my patch, I wanted to go and have a look. I wanted to understand how this thing could have happened. On the way, I was stopped by one of your colleagues. I remember, he had stripes ...'

Probably that cocksure lieutenant who had described his version of events a year earlier on the beach ... Didier M went on, 'He asked me for my ID, but unfortunately I didn't have my papers on me. I told him I was the cook at the Emmaüs community of Le Relecq-Kerhuon. He told me to beat it. I took a little detour and then I went to the beach. There were bloodstains. It was upsetting. Looking at them, I said to myself that the murderer must have been spattered. I also thought that the murderer must have watched the woman from the spot where I sit and have a drink. Just above. That woman … the killer "wanted" her. I don't know why, but I'm sure he did.'

'When you arrived at the beach, didn't you see the Keep Out signs?'

'I didn't see the red and yellow tapes straight away, because I took a little path that leads directly to the scene. It's on your left when you're facing the sea. Then it was too late …'

'What did you do next?'

'I went back to the community for lunch. I met the director and told him everything I've just told you. He lectured me and told me not to hang around the murder scene again.'

The interview was over. I had no intention of raising the Heaulme question again. I didn't want Didier M to know that I was interested in 'big Francis', as I had come to call him. There was a chance that they might meet again. Vagrants often bump into each other in the course of their travels.

Before releasing Didier M from custody, I telephoned Bertrand in Brest and asked him if he wouldn't mind running a quick check on the cook's statement. Two hours later, he called me back. He had just interviewed Daniel, Didier M's mate, as well as the owner of the Longchamp bar. The two men corroborated our witness's claims. Cleared of any suspicion, the witness was released. His interview was useful. I was now certain that 'The Gaul' was not a fabrication. Furthermore, he had been in the vicinity of the beach on the eve of the murder.

To follow up this lead, I needed another spell at Rosny-sous-Bois, where I would surely find out more about this man with a particularly apt nickname.

Once again, Serge L assisted me in my research. For hours on end, we cross-referenced every possible record. Philippe D, alias 'The Gaul', had not come to official attention for years. I didn't learn much from the study of old court proceedings. Impossible to find a recent address. He had been on the road for twenty years. He was a loner, with no family, and no apparent friends. No useful leads ... This was not the way to track down this key witness. His name was circulated on the wanted for questioning list, but I hoped to avoid having to wait until by some lucky coincidence he was stopped by police. If 'The Gaul' was settled at the moment, months, even years, could go by before he was stopped by a patrol.

There might be another solution. A computer search of the national database of individuals wanted by the police yielded some valuable information. The computer stores the dates of identity checks on a person for two years. Although it came up with nothing for 'The Gaul', the printer sprang into action for Francis Heaulme, producing a listing of several pages detailing more than sixty dates, with a note of the exact time and the police unit that had carried out the check. An amazing itinerary emerged. Francis Heaulme was constantly on the move. It was almost beyond belief: between the months of April and May alone of that year, 1990, he had passed through Cambrai, Lunéville, Metz, Pont-à-Mousson, Verdun, Lens, Berck-sur-Saens, Trouville-sur-Mer, Mortain, Lanmeur, Lorient, Tarnos and Bayonne.

Fourteen towns in eleven different *départements* stretching from north to south and east to west of the country. With what I believed I knew about the man, this odyssey was a cause for concern. How many other victims had he left in his wake?

But that August 1990, the whereabouts of 'The Gaul' were still unknown, and for the time being he was the only witness able to influence the course of events. In Rennes, the situation was hardly any better. Our boss had been replaced. The new commander of the criminal investigation unit, Colonel F, had taken up his post and reorganised the section. Major JR was appointed second in command. He was now my immediate superior. Changes soon followed. My superiors asked me to 'consider concluding my investigation'. Meanwhile I was given other cases, in particular a murder in the Nantes region which was going to take up nearly all of my time. Now, I had no choice but to grin and bear it. I would just have to wait until 'The Gaul' was miraculously stopped. But I had no intention of closing the case so abruptly, and neither did the investigating magistrate. Whatever the outcome, Francis Heaulme had to be questioned. Another year was to go by.

It was not until 1991 that hope revived. One morning, Serge L called me from Rosny-sous-Bois.

'Your "Gaul" was in Bayonne last week, are you interested?'

Was I interested! ... I rushed in to see Colonel F.

'Colonel, I think we've found the crucial witness we've been looking for in the Moulin Blanc case. He's known as "The Gaul". Heaulme mentioned him during an interview. He's been located in Bayonne and I'd like to pay him a visit.'

Major JR cut me short.

'You're not going to tell me that you suspect Heaulme in this investigation! I was with you when we had him in custody. It's not him, and you know it. Why don't you come clean and tell me you just fancy a trip to Bayonne?'

Before I could open my mouth, the Colonel went on, 'Abgrall, you'll stay put and wind up this case as soon as possible.'

Flabbergasted, I just stood there speechless. Once again I was up against general scepticism and military discipline. Had Francis Heaulme pulled the wool over JR's eyes so cleverly that he had absolutely no doubts? Once again, my hopes were dashed. I didn't see how I was going to be able to nail the suspect. Meanwhile, Heaulme continued his travels.

December arrived. Serge L had left Rosny-sous-Bois several months earlier. His replacement was equally helpful. He informed me that Francis Heaulme was in Bischwiller, in Alsace. He was working in a rehabilitation association. As I had to hand in my report before long, I decided to do one last thing. On the morning of the 17th I found myself standing in front of a small, three-storey apartment block in Bischwiller, along with the gendarme Éric C from Brest.

'Big Francis' was sharing the apartment of a partially disabled young woman. This building stood at the end of a little cul de sac, in a quiet, isolated spot. I was amazed. Had Heaulme changed so much that he had settled down?

It was 10 a.m. when I knocked on his door. Francis Heaulme opened it a fraction. He was surprised, but seemed pleased to see me and he invited me in. The one-room flat was microscopic. It was very neat. A big bed took up half of the room. This bed was arranged in a strange manner: the sheets were rumpled on either side whereas the centre was perfectly smooth, without a crease ... If Francis and his lady friend were sleeping together, it was far apart, avoiding contact.

'Francis,' I said, 'we're going to have to have another talk about your movements ... but before we do, we're going to search through your belongings again.'

The search yielded nothing. No weapon. No bloodstained clothing. No correspondence referring to the murder, no giveaway press cuttings which killers often collect ... We discreetly left his home in the little apartment building. No point alerting the neighbours. The interview with our witness was going to take place at the Strasbourg gendarmerie.

We installed ourselves in a soulless office that was as neutral as possible. Everything in it was of a professional nature. Here, nothing would disturb us. The confrontation had only just begun when the pressure set in. This man had an incredible faculty for creating a climate of violence. He knew what we were going to be talking about and his face was transformed – his features stiff, his lips clamped together and his stare often too piercing to meet. His body also changed. Every one of his muscles seemed to contract. At times like that, he really did remind me of a wild animal about to pounce. Perhaps his expression and attitude were linked to his concentration, I don't know. In any case, they did not perturb me any more.

The chief who was with me watched him, then signalled his unease. I indicated that everything was fine and I whispered that this behaviour was usual in Francis Heaulme. The interview began.

'Francis, I've checked out what you told me in Normandy. There are some things that don't add up at all ... Do you remember what you told me?'

Once again, his eyes bored into mine. Again, he spoke in a mechanical, stilted manner. He launched into a series of wild explanations.

'I told you a load of rubbish. I lied. About the army, none of that was true. I was declared unfit for service because of my eyesight. And what I told you about attacking that woman on the beach, I made that up too, and there's no such person as Henri L ... I lied to you because I was afraid, I wanted to protect myself. I do sometimes think about the Moulin Blanc murder. I've even thought, in my dreams, that it was me. But I was in hospital in Quimper on Sunday 14 May 1989. I didn't leave the hospital, even if I have the feeling I went to the beach that day. I only found out what had happened in the papers, the next day, the Monday, when I was at Quimper station. It upset me because the day before, on Saturday 13, I had gone for a walk in that exact spot.'

His words came out in a single burst, the rhythm and the tone completely flat. He didn't move a muscle, kept his fists clenched all the time, and never took his eyes off mine. He clearly had not

changed. I didn't know what to do. I had no evidence to con-
front him with, yet above all I couldn't let on how weak the case
was. I tried another tactic.

'Francis, have you been in hospital anywhere else, apart from
Quimper?'

'Yes, I've had several stays in psychiatric hospitals. I've even
had several treatments for alcoholism. I thought I was cured …
That's all I have to say.'

It was 5 p.m. I knew what those words meant. There was no
point pressing him. There was nothing more to be done. Driving him back to home to Bischwiller, I asked him to talk about
his 'little cock-ups'. Francis was on his guard, I knew, but I think
he liked talking to me.

'I cocked up a few times it's true, but I'm cured. Now I've
got a fiancée and everything's fine.'

'How did you meet her?'

'I was working as a labourer and my girlfriend happened to
come past. It was love at first sight. We saw each other again and
she asked me to come and live in her flat. She said that God had
placed me on her path. She's very religious, we go and sing in
the church choir.'

'How long have you been together?'

'Since May 1991.'

In my mind I saw that double bed where each stayed on their
own side. Francis Heaulme's lack of sexuality worried me.
Couldn't that be at the root of his problems, of his terrible violence? Could it not simply be the motive for the murders I suspected him of? I felt sure that I was sitting with the killer.

When we got back, Francis's girlfriend was at home. She was a small, dark-haired woman in her thirties, barely one metre sixty but very stout. Due to her disability, she could not manage on her own, and received a certain amount of support. She was smiling, and wore a woollen hat pulled down over her ears. This woman was particularly sweet-natured, and I couldn't help thinking what an odd couple they made. I tried to talk to her to find out whether Francis had confided in her. Visibly, she knew nothing. I hoped she was not in danger.

Before taking my leave, I caught Francis by the arm and marched him into the corridor. He was taken aback. I acted like him, showing no feelings. Speaking in a calm voice, without aggression and looking deep into his eyes, I said, 'Francis, I know what you've done. I'll be back, and next time you'll be leaving with me. You will go either to prison, or to a psychiatric hospital if that's what you need. Meanwhile, go and seek medical help and stop all this.'

He didn't bat an eyelid, then replied, 'François, you'd make a good psychiatrist!'

It wasn't the first time he'd compared me to a psychiatrist ... Coming from a man like him, what should I make of this? Was it sincere or cynical? We parted on a handshake, as evasive as ever.

Before setting off home, I recorded my conversations with Francis Heaulme. For the last time I informed my Strasbourg colleagues of the suspicions hanging over this man and warned them about his strange behaviour. I didn't think I would ever be coming back here. I was tiring of this investigation, almost defeated. Francis would never talk and I would never have the proof I needed to nail him.

In Rennes, my lack of success prompted Major JR to demand I close the case. I was devastated. It was Christmas, and I went on holiday. On 26 December, at lunchtime, the phone rang in my house on the Breton coast, overlooking the Atlantic.

'This is François, from the Brest criminal investigation unit. I want to let you know that "The Gaul" has just been arrested in Bourges. They're expecting you there. Off you go.'

This was perhaps my last chance. I could fit in a lightning holiday … I left for Bourges, accompanied by a colleague.

The local gendarmes were not used to criminal cases, and they were pleased to see us. On our arrival, we learned that 'The Gaul' was panic-stricken when he heard that Breton investigators were coming to interview him. He kept repeating, 'I'm going to take the rap for someone else, I'm going to take the rap for someone else. I've never been to Brittany … I'm fucked, I'm going to take the rap for someone else!'

It was 9.30 p.m. when the interview began. Two colleagues from Bourges were present. Before my arrival, they had talked to 'The Gaul' at length. They were going to be useful to me. Philippe D, the key witness, was at last sitting opposite me. He was a short, slim man of forty-five; he looked just like Asterix with his blond whiskers, except for his blue anorak.

His fear was almost tangible, verging on panic, which is

unusual in this type of character. Life on the road tends to harden men, and as someone who had been raised in care institutions, he must have experienced far more distressing situations.

As usual, I began with his life story, a soft tactic which is tried and tested and reveals the little bargains with reality, the periods over which the interviewee prefers to draw a veil.

'Tell me about your itinerary over these last few years.'

'For three years, I've been staying in Emmaüs communities. I haven't moved around much, I stay put for several months. The place I stayed longest was Poitiers. I spent a year there. I've stayed in the communities in Limoges, Poitiers and Bourges, that's all. I'm sure, yes, sure … I stopped drinking eleven years ago. Actually, I haven't drunk since I was convicted for the old woman business. All I remember about that is that a mate broke down a door and ran off. And I got sent down for it.'

I sensed that it was going to be hard to gain his confidence, and harder still to obtain any useful information.

After each sentence, almost with each word he spoke to me, 'The Gaul' looked imploringly at my two colleagues who kept repeating, 'Don't be afraid. It's simple, if you haven't done anything, nothing will happen to you.'

This little game was leading nowhere. I stopped beating about the bush.

'Are you quite certain you haven't stayed in any other Emmaüs communities than the ones you mentioned?'

'No, no, I'm sure.'

'Didn't you go to Brittany?'

'Oh no, I didn't go there!'

'Do you know where Brittany is?'

'It's the sea,' he replied edgily. 'I've stayed here all the time, I haven't moved. I don't move from my patch.'

'Will you still say you've never been to Brittany if we talk to you about Brest or Le Relecq-Kerhuon?'

'I've never been there, I tell you. I swear it!'

'The Gaul' was ashen, his eyes evasive. I stopped talking at that point and looked at one of the two gendarmes, who went on, 'Philippe, look how fat his dossier is, he's checked everything. If he's asking you the question, there's a reason for it, so be careful.'

I could feel that 'The Gaul' was at the end of his tether. After a few moments' silence, he finally decided to talk.

'It's true, I was there,' he admitted in a whisper. 'It's an Emmaüs community near the beach, outside Brest. I stayed there for two months. I did carpentry there. I didn't have any friends, I minded my own business ...'

'Why didn't you want to talk about Brest?'

'Because I don't like the place. There was a bad atmosphere in the community. That was because some of them drank.'

Philippe D was beginning to open up a little. 'The Gaul' had been mulling over this business for months. Apart from the pressure of the interview, he had a real need to unburden himself.

'On the Sunday, first of all I went for a half at the café by the beach. Then I bought a bottle of beer at the grocery near the old boat in the port. On the way back to the community, I stopped near the beach to drink my beer.'

'Can you describe the place where you drank your beer?'

'You had to go through some bushes. And then, go down over some big rocks on the pebble beach. It's a quiet place and I drank my beer there.'

'After leaving the Emmaüs community at Le Relecq-Kerhuon, where did you go?'

'I slept rough, in the bushes, near the place where I drank my beers. I stayed there for several days …'

'Did anybody from the community come and visit you in your bushes and share a drink with you?'

'Yes, mates came to see me. I can't remember their names.'

It was 11.30 p.m., we broke off for a sandwich and to put our heads together. We all agreed that 'The Gaul' was still keeping something from us. If he seemed more relaxed, it was only on the surface. Certain questions completely fazed him. This man had been on the beach at the time of the murder. He was in the habit of drinking his beer in the spot where, shortly before the murder, a witness saw a man in a blue anorak sitting. The same garment that 'The Gaul' was still wearing. He had some important things to tell us, that was certain.

At half past midnight, the interview resumed. We spoke for another half an hour or so, then I decided to show him the photograph album. He recognised Heaulme, then Didier M.

'The first one's an alcoholic. I saw him in the community and he came to see me in the bushes. He drank a lot and turned very nasty afterwards. Didier, the other guy, was a mate.'

'Did Heaulme talk about women, and if he did, in what way?'

'He talked about them a lot, he wanted to screw them all. He looked at women in a weird way, but in any case, with his looks, his glasses ... He was a really strange character, he talked to himself. He's a sadist.'

'And what happened the last time you were with him?'

A leaden silence. 'The Gaul' suddenly stopped in mid-flow, but my colleague encouraged him to reply. He was persuasive, and our witness continued.

'All right. This time I'll tell you the whole story. I was in the bushes, just above the beach, as I told you. Heaulme arrived wearing jeans and a white sports shirt ... He'd drunk half a litre of red wine ... He was very worked up. I don't know why. Then we climbed down over the rocks near the bushes onto the beach ... There was a woman sunbathing there, she was wearing a bikini ... He started heading towards her. I followed him for about ten metres. Heaulme had gone sort of crazy. I thought he was going to rape her so I followed to stop him. When the woman saw him coming, she sat up on her towel. She was scared. Still sitting there, she asked what he wanted. He said, "I'm going to screw you." The woman got up and grabbed Heaulme by the shoulders, and he seized her throat. He squeezed her throat with one hand. I didn't intervene, because Heaulme said to me nastily, "Why are you following me?" The woman began to scream and I ran away ... I went to the station and got on the first train to Paris. I was scared. That's all I saw ... I went to Tours ... I saw on the news that a woman had been stabbed to death in Brest. I saw pictures of the murder scene and I recognised the place where Heaulme had attacked the woman. I knew it was him, but I thought he'd been caught. I was scared of being accused of the killing but I had nothing to do with it.

That's why I was afraid to talk to you. One last thing, I was wearing a blue anorak that day. Now I've told you everything.'

It was 3.30 a.m. After two years of investigations, 'The Gaul' had finally spilled his secret. We quickly completed the remaining formalities, and Philippe D picked out Aline Pérès from a number of photos of women. The customary search yielded nothing of relevance and 'The Gaul' was released. With the agreement of the investigating magistrate, he promised not to leave Bourges, so that he would be able to respond if summonsed. I felt relieved, but I couldn't help thinking how unwittingly selfish this man had been. If he had come forward on the day of the murder, other lives would certainly have been saved.

5

Confessions

It was the beginning of 1992. Francis Heaulme was under discreet surveillance by the Bischwiller gendarmerie. Their only orders were not to let him take to the road again. In the meantime, at Le Relecq-Kerhuon, 'The Gaul's' statement had been meticulously checked. Everything he had said tallied. We were ready for another meeting with our man.

On 6 January at 8 a.m., Éric C, the Brest investigator who had accompanied me on my first trip to Alsace, joined me in Rennes. Before we left for Strasbourg, I called the chief at Avignon. He had made no headway with his investigation. Two and a half years on, and the case of the murdered former legionnaire in Courthézon was still unsolved. When we invited him to come to Bischwiller with us, he declined. He was not interested in meeting our suspect.

It was nearly midnight by the time we arrived at the hotel in

Bischwiller. We'd nearly got stuck in the snow on the little country roads of Alsace. During this long journey, we had had plenty of time to think about the interview and discuss the case in minute detail. Anxious not to get caught up in Heaulme's little games, I reminded Éric how lucid his ramblings were. We both agreed to play by his rules. We would let him take the initiative and lead us into his world.

The next morning, we visited Francis. We listened quietly outside the door of his studio apartment: somebody was home. I knocked. No reply. But we could hear a person moving around inside. I knocked again and Heaulme's voice at last replied, 'Who is it?'

I answered, 'It's Jean-François!'

He appeared in the doorway.

'It's you?' he said, relieved. 'Come in!'

As I stepped inside, I glimpsed him putting something down in a corner. I quickly examined the room. Nothing appeared to have changed since my last visit. Heaulme planted himself in front of us and challenged me.

'You allowed me to enjoy Christmas?'

The game was on. I answered, 'I told you I'd be back. Did you have a good Christmas, at least?'

Each eyed the other searchingly. We were both concealing our hand. Now it was a matter of waiting to see who would give his game away first.

'While I was waiting for you, I went to see the sea. Yes, I went to see the sea,' he repeated, his eyes boring into mine.

I didn't understand what he meant. Those staring eyes. I

didn't reply, this wasn't the time or the place to open the interview.

'Francis, we're going to leave now, pack your bag.'

As we were about to leave the apartment, I noticed a hatchet behind the door. Was that the object he'd been putting away – or hiding – when we arrived? I feigned surprise:

'Francis, why have you got a hatchet in your apartment?'

'I'm having problems with some Turks. There are lots of Turks here. They're foreigners and I don't like foreigners. And my girlfriend locked me up in the flat. With that, she wouldn't dare do it again. Anyway, I climb out and go over the rooftops.'

His words were as disconcerting as ever. We left for Strasbourg. So as to preserve the strange rapport that had developed between us, I decided not to handcuff him. The two of us were sitting in the back of a little grey Peugeot 205, and Francis seemed happy. What could he have up his sleeve?'

He talked non-stop all through the thirty-minute journey, carefully weighing each word.

'Before I was with my girlfriend, I had a few cock-ups. You know, François, I was ill, alcoholic, but now I'm OK.'

I listened without replying, or pointing out that he still kept getting my name wrong. If he preferred to call me François, what did it matter? It was a name that sounded like his own, and if that made it easier for him to talk ...

10 a.m. We were back in our office at the Strasbourg gendarmerie. Although not completely relaxed, Francis was less tense than he had been during our previous confrontations. I opened the conversation.

'Francis, here's your notification that you are being held for questioning. You have already been interviewed twice in this investigation, now you only have to spend another twenty-eight hours with me. You know, that's not much time to talk about your problems. If you want me to help you, you mustn't keep making things up. Just tell me what you've been doing, exactly as things happened. That way, I'll be able to explain that you're a different man now from the one I met on the roads of Normandy. Talk to me about the people you've met too, people who've made a special impression, anything you like ...'

I had no idea whether this invitation to talk about himself would have any impact on Heaulme. Maybe that was up to the psychiatrists. How far was he a dangerous manipulator? Right then, all I wanted was to get him to speak. This new interview was crucial. I had to play it tight. As usual, Francis had not taken his eyes off me. He began:

'This time, I'm determined to explain things. This business is getting me down, and it's been going round and round in my mind since May 1989. At that time, I was a sick alcoholic and very dangerous. I was also very excitable. Since 1987, I'd been living in Emmaüs communities. Actually, I fell ill after my mother's death in 1984 ... I've travelled all over France ... Between September and November 1990, I even went to Spain.'

He soon got round to his stay in Brittany. He was under control, watching our movements. Éric and I remained impassive. He went on:

'I liked going to Brest because I love warships. In fact, I'm fascinated by war. I've watched lots of war films ... What I like about them are the close-combat scenes, hand-to-hand fighting. The weapon I like best is the knife.'

He paused, his gaze still riveted on me. I had already experienced this. Without looking away, I waited.

'My third trip to Brittany was back in May 1989 ... That time I stayed in the Emmaüs community just outside Brest by the Moulin Blanc beach. Something happened there.'

He stopped again, then resumed:

'I caught a fellow in my room who said he was a stretcher-bearer. He was searching through my things. I got angry and ... I took 100 francs from him. With that money, I got pissed. I went to the beach, as far as the white boat lying high and dry there. I lay down beside the boat and I thought about a murder scene with a knife on a woman. I imagined a man stabbing a woman on the beach. Once I was feeling a bit better, I went back up to the community, picked up my bag and left. I hitch-hiked to Quimper. I was picked up straight away by a young man who dropped me off on the edge of town. Then I asked someone if there was a hospital nearby ... That person took me to the hospital. I complained of a heart problem. I was admitted to casualty and then transferred to cardiology. I was put in a room with an elderly man. I was put on a drip.'

He fell silent. Sensing a mounting tension, I went to get some coffees from the lounge. There, two colleagues from Strasbourg hailed me.

'We saw your customer getting out of the car in the yard, he looks like an odd character. How's it going?'

I replied with a faint smile, 'He's strange, yes. But for the time being, we're making slow progress. He's telling us about himself. We haven't got down to the nitty gritty yet.'

I went out with my three coffees. These little breaks often helped ease the atmosphere. Once we'd drained our cups, we were ready to pursue the conversation.

'Francis,' I said, 'shall we go on?'

His expression became detached again and he continued his tale where he'd left off, in the same monotone.

'I spent the night in hospital, and the next morning I asked them to remove the drip. And they did. In my mind, I was still thinking about the murder scene I'd imagined the day before. I can't remember if I had lunch in the hospital, but what I am sure of is that I left the hospital. I was wearing a white sports shirt and shorts. I was also wearing trainers. I didn't tell anyone I was leaving the hospital. Anyway, nobody tried to stop me. I was still thinking about the murder I'd dreamed about and besides, I wanted to get my own back on the stretcher-bearer. So I planned to go to Brest. I was mad, I saw red. I had my knife with me. I put it in my shorts pocket. It's a knife with a wooden handle, and the end of the blade is broken. I broke it while I was working at the Emmaüs. The blade folds into the handle. When I left the hospital, I made for the expressway into Brest. I hitch-hiked. Again, I got a lift straight away. The driver, a young man, even dropped me off at Moulin Blanc beach. As soon as I arrived, I went to this sort of grocery-café that's not far from the boat lying high and dry on the beach. There, I drank some of the bottle of beer I'd bought. I was still thinking about the murder I'd imagined, and I was very wound up. I drank half the bottle by the boat. I wasn't drunk, but I was wound up. I walked down by the water, towards the bridge. I walked for nearly a kilo-metre. I was still thinking about the murder. I walked to the rocks going towards the bridge, after the car park. Actually, they're stones placed up against the wall. When I got there, I saw a man with fair hair sitting on the top of the stones. I knew his face from the bar near the car park. I don't know his name, but he had shoulder-length hair.'

Francis observed our reaction. I took advantage of this brief pause to show him the photo album of witnesses.

'Is there a photo of this person in the album?'

Amused, he studied each face carefully, making the odd com-ment as he turned the pages.

'That one I met in Châteauroux, and him in Bayonne.'

He didn't stop at his own picture, but did however pause at the sight of another.

'It's him, it's the man in photo number sixty-six.'

He was pointing at the portrait of 'The Gaul'. It all seemed to fit together. We had to be careful not to make any blunders that would destroy the tenuous bond we had built up. We made no comment; I simply named Philippe D.

Heaulme went on, 'As I said, "The Gaul" was sitting up on the rocks. He was looking at a woman, a beautiful woman who was sunbathing. She was wearing a bikini … She was lying on a towel … I didn't like the way Philippe D was staring at this woman. I was still thinking about my murder dream. I stood at the foot of the sea wall.'

His lips were pinched and his face twisted into a grimace. He stiffened. Then I asked him whether he would find it easier to draw a rough sketch. Éric gave him a piece of paper and a pen. With astonishing application, Francis drew the beach and the surrounding roads. He located the grocer's, the boat, the car park, the café and the rocks. Further away, he added the Emmaüs community and the road bridge leading towards Quimper.

I interrupted him, 'Fine Francis, but where were you and the others?'

Then he added little crosses to the diagram, explaining, 'I was there, by the boat, and there was a fisherman here. After the car park, near the rocks, there was the fair-haired fellow, the woman, and me.'

'What time was this?'

Heaulme did not reply, but wrote '5–5.30 p.m.' on his drawing.

'Excellent Francis, now write your name and sign it, and the drawing will be filed with your interview. It's easier that way, isn't it?'

Francis nodded and seemed satisfied. Although he had just located the exact position of the victim on the beach, and that of the two men spotted by the boy at the time of the murder, Éric and I chose not to show any reaction. We were especially anxious not to let on what we were hoping to get out of him, so as not to reveal the holes in our case. Our suspect had to be kept in a state of uncertainty. Besides, I still had a hunch that the murder on that spring Sunday in 1989 was not Heaulme's first. Perhaps he would talk about his other killings.

It was 1.30 p.m. I suggested that the three of us go out for lunch. This surprised Francis and amused Éric. A table was reserved in the gendarmerie canteen.

Ten minutes later we entered the restaurant, 300 metres from the office block. At that hour, the place was almost empty, and the few people left were finishing their dessert. Francis, in a purple tracksuit, caused a few smiles, to which he replied with a cheery 'Hello'. We seated ourselves at a little table in a corner of the room, as secluded as possible. The manager did not know that the man with us was in custody. The dish of the day was sauerkraut. We were served immediately. We were about to eat when Francis asked out of the blue, 'François, have you met "The Gaul"?'

I told him I had.

'What did he tell you?'

'What do you think he might have told me?'

'That it was me. He told you it was me.'

Éric and I made no reply. Just then an officer came and sat at our table. There was a spare place. We then witnessed a surreal scene. Unfazed, Heaulme went on talking.

'I grabbed my knife and slit her throat, then I stuck the blade into her ribs. She looked nice.'

The gendarme froze, and gave an awkward smile. Heaulme went on, 'I was ill, I didn't want to, but I stabbed her all the same.'

At these words, the gendarme rose from the table and retreated to the back of the room. Given the awkwardness this was causing, I suggested to Francis Heaulme that we continue the conversation back in our office. Too late, the manager was already there, followed by the gendarme.

'Who is this gentleman?' he asked.

'He's with us. For the time being, he's being held for questioning. But we'll be leaving very shortly, don't worry.'

The gendarme insisted, 'He's mad, he can't stay here.'

The manager glanced at Francis and urged us to leave. 'Now!'

Not perturbed in the least, Francis Heaulme carried on tucking into his sauerkraut as if nothing were amiss. As for the gendarme, he abruptly left the canteen. It was too much for him.

2.30 p.m. Back in the office, Éric went and got some coffees and I was left alone with Francis. His attitude in the canteen had surprised me, for he had given himself away. Nevertheless, he always knew what line to take with any questioner. He adjusted quickly and was always in control of himself. He could have explained this business from the start, but had preferred to shelter behind his dreams ... No doubt less incoherent than they sounded. What a devious character! And what lay beneath this lack of emotion which we were trying to mimic?

I listened to him.

'I don't know, François, I've had enough of this business. I can't remember a thing any more.'

'I'll help you, Francis. When you arrived on the beach, you were thinking of something, so try and remember. Try and get it all straight. Talk to me, I'm listening to you, even if at the moment what I'm typing has nothing to do with the case, it's just standard information, custody formalities. So take your time and talk to me as things go through your mind. You'll see, it will all come back to you.'

Concentrating on the keyboard, I spoke without looking at him.

'At the time, I was ill. I had fits. I would feel one coming on. I walked fast. Nobody could keep up with me. I can walk for whole days … My veins swell and I go rigid. I'm afraid of nobody, I can fight three men. I see red. I can taste blood in my mouth.'

He now seemed to be finding it hard to talk. I looked up. His voice had abruptly changed, and now he was speaking in the present tense. Sitting opposite me was no longer Francis, but a tormented man whose face was contorted into a terrifying grimace. His eyes were so bloodshot that the whites no longer showed. He kept opening and closing his fists, making his veins swell. He was tense, rigid. He was terrifying to look at. I had the impression that he was literally about to pounce. I leaped over the desk and caught him by the arm.

'Francis! Relax … We're going to go for a little walk,' I said, pulling him up from his chair.

He was no longer breathing regularly, but was panting hard. In this state, we walked up and down the corridors. He took huge, mechanical strides, forcing me to trot to keep up with him. I didn't loosen my grip. Éric was right behind me, just in case. After five minutes of this 'walk', which felt endless, his face finally relaxed. Francis Heaulme collected himself. We asked if he wanted to see a doctor. He refused – 'I'm not asking for anything at all!'

I didn't press the point. We would resume the interview later. To my great surprise, Francis became even more forthcoming.

'At the foot of the rocks, I waved to Philippe D to come and join me. The woman wasn't taking any notice of us. She was about ten metres away ... I was very wound up. I told him what I'd seen in my murder dream. He told me I was nuts and to bugger off. Actually, "The Gaul" talked about the woman who was sunbathing. He said, "She's all right, isn't she! I bet you couldn't go up and talk to her." I thought about my dream and I opened my knife. It was in my pocket. I walked towards her with my hands behind my back, holding the knife. I knew that this woman was going to be attacked. When she saw me, she got up. She could see what was going to happen. She saw the knife. I said to her, "My name's Francis Heaulme. I've got a problem, I want to talk to you. I dreamed you were going to be stabbed." The woman answered, "You stink of alcohol. Go away!" she also said, "Leave! or I'll scream." The woman was scared and she screamed. Just then, Philippe D came over and I had my fit. I grabbed the woman by the neck and I stabbed her three or four times with my knife. I stabbed hard, I felt my knife touch the bone. I was out of control. I heard "The Gaul" shout … but I carried on stabbing the woman …'

I interrupted. 'Francis, do you remember how you placed your hands around the woman's throat?'

'Yes, very clearly.'

I asked him to repeat the gesture on Éric.

'But gently, OK?'

In an instant, Heaulme grabbed my partner by the throat. He only needed to squeeze a little harder to leave the same finger and nail marks as those found on Aline Pérès's neck. Slowly, he withdrew his hand. He carried on:

'Philippe, "The Gaul", cleared off. I've never seen him again. I couldn't move. The woman was lying at my feet. She wasn't dead. She was looking me straight in the eyes. I think her carotid had burst. It was an accident, this business …'

I let him describe his horrific crime. The coldly recorded details would serve as proof at the trial.

It was 4 p.m., the interview was over. Francis was very calm, as if unaware of the gravity of his declarations. For my part, I felt relieved to have taken things to their logical conclusion. The answer was hidden behind the last card. That night, Aline Pérès's murderer would sleep behind bars. The first night of a long spell in prison, in all probability. The satisfaction of a job well done is relative, for it implies more suffering for another family. The Moulin Blanc killer would now be locked up, shut away from the world.

His appearance before the Strasbourg prosecutor was set for 6 p.m. the same day. Meanwhile, the three of us went to the lounge. The officer from the local criminal investigation unit, Jean-Louis B, was with us. He had been assigned to our case. It was the second time he had met Francis here. He was familiar with our investigation and asked me if we had finished. Francis did not give me time to reply, but said, 'Yes, it was me, but it was an accident. I've explained it all to François and Éric.'

Jean-Louis went on, 'And what about Avignon?'

To our amazement, Heaulme replied, 'That was me too! There I used a big stone to crush his head.'

This new admission came like a bolt from the blue. I was speechless. But this confession could not be included in the case I was handling. Officially, I was only mandated for the Moulin Blanc murder. How could we go about endorsing any further declarations? If Francis was ready to talk, we could not record him. Only the investigator from Avignon was legally entitled to do so. We contacted him at once, but he refused to come. The excuse he gave – that he would interview Heaulme once he was behind bars – seemed feeble. As investigators, we knew he was taking a very big risk. This situation might never arise again.

Jean-Louis left us for a moment and returned with another investigator. They questioned Francis about Avignon. Amused by the situation, Francis confirmed his initial account. They decided to draw up a statement, even if it had no legal status.

Other investigators came into the lounge discussing their cases. Francis, absorbed in drinking an orange juice, seemed oblivious to what was going on around him. However, he did react to the remark by one colleague. 'I'm having a problem with some Turks and a series of burglaries,' said the gendarme. 'They won't admit anything, even though they are in possession of stolen goods.'

Francis put down his plastic cup and without the slightest hesitation offered to help. 'Do you want me to get them to talk? I can come with you!'

The situation was almost comic, but everyone remained serious.

'No, thank you,' replied the gendarme, surprised and embarrassed.

5.30 p.m. Now it was time to go to the Law Courts. We clambered back into the unmarked Peugeot 205 placed at our disposal. Éric drove, Jean-Louis sat in front and Francis and I were a bit squashed in the back – Heaulme was nearly two metres tall. This time, he was handcuffed. He had agreed without a fuss.

An escort was waiting for us in front of the Law Courts. We handed over our prisoner. In a few moments he would be brought before the investigating magistrate, who would notify him of his arrest. We hastily said goodbye.

Strasbourg was simply a stage where Heaulme was in transit. In less than a week, he would be in Brest prison. There, experts would study his case, there would doubtless be more conversations. I hoped to be able to understand the man he was inside. How many other murders had he committed? Other women? Men? Children? Where, when, and above all, why? I was still far from knowing all the answers.

PART TWO

Dangerous liaisons

6

True and false faces of Heaulme

A little get-together was organised on my return to Rennes. My colleagues had booked a dining room in an Alsatian brasserie, and I contributed a few bottles of wine from the Strasbourg region. It's a tradition to celebrate the end of an investigation in this manner.

Everybody was at this dinner, even Major JR. The atmosphere was friendly and relaxed. My colleagues presented me with a cork notice board covered with various references to the investigation. A white windmill made out of card symbolising Moulin Blanc was pinned to the centre of the board, and there was an hourglass full of red sand as a reminder of the slowness of the investigation, and the Opinel knife which I never found. It was a nice gesture, a way of gently turning the page. But during the months to come, I was unlikely to forget the mysterious Francis Heaulme. Quite the opposite.

It was the end of January 1992, and I was utterly convinced that Francis Heaulme was the author of a series of murders. I circulated a memo to this effect all over the country. Responses soon came pouring in. Several requests for information landed on my desk. They came from regional police stations or gendarmeries investigating homicides. They all wanted to know the itinerary of Aline Pérès's murderer. There was a prospect of further meetings with this elusive man.

I was far from displeased. In fact, I was keen to resume our strange conversations. I wanted to understand why he killed. I didn't think his crimes were motiveless. Something was at the root of his murderous impulses, but what?

I was no longer dealing with the Moulin Blanc case, but I could talk to Francis Heaulme about other matters. Before embarking on a new round of interviews, I set up a meeting with the presiding magistrate.

Reconstructed after World War Two, like the rest of the city, the Brest Law Courts are a single block. Several storeys high, this granite building overlooks the docks. It was here that the investigating magistrate awaited me on the morning of 27 March 1992. This discreet, almost self-effacing local man, appointed only three years earlier, had just turned thirty. The Moulin Blanc murder was his first big criminal case, but he was well aware of the unusual nature of it. He knew that Aline Pérès's murderer was no ordinary killer. He greeted me with an affable smile as I entered the long, narrow space of his dingy little office.

'I have come to ask you for authorisation to contact other criminal investigation units,' I said. 'Since his arrest, Francis Heaulme has caught the attention of a number of investigators and they would like to interview him.'

'There's no problem,' he replied. 'Come this afternoon at 2 p.m. if you like. I'm drafting his personal history. Only, you're going to have to wait.'

I agreed.

2 p.m. At the Law Courts, Francis Heaulme was brought in by two officers. As he was about to go into the judge's chamber, he spotted me in the corridor and shot me a little smile. I tagged on behind the escort. Heaulme and his lawyer took their places facing the magistrate. An officer removed the accused's handcuffs and joined me by the door where I was sitting.

Francis did not take much notice of his counsel. He knew that the charges would not be brought up. According to procedure, this was just a matter of summing up his itinerary and recording the names of all those he wished to call as witnesses, in particular character witnesses. Covering his private life, family, social, school and work life etc., the personal history is meant to reflect a person's character. It is also a vital stage; through his choices and omissions, the criminal's true and false faces emerge.

After reminding him of the object of the cross-examination, the judge invited him to describe the stages of his life. Francis Heaulme enjoyed this part. He liked being the centre of attention. He began his story in his stilted voice, his eyes boring into the magistrate's:

'My father used to beat my mother all the time. I would step in between them to stop him hitting her. My father told me it was my fault my mother died ... I got on very well with her. But my father used to beat me. Once, when I was eighteen, I was very frightened. He took me down to the cellar and hit me with his belt on the left shoulder because he wanted to beat my mother and I'd interfered. He collected military weapons, and I'd picked up a bayonet from a case hanging on the wall, and told him to stop ...'

I recalled our first meeting. Then too, he had talked of violence, war and trauma. Was it all true, or was this some new fabrication? Whichever it was, when he spoke about his father, he seemed on the point of exploding. His tone was furious and his words rapped out like lashes of a whip. He went on:

'Life at home was very hard. My mother was very unhappy with my father, and so was my sister. We weren't allowed to do anything, we couldn't go out. My mother didn't want us to hang around with the local kids because there were a lot of delinquents in the area ... When my father turned round and said it was my fault my mother was dead, I tried to commit suicide by stabbing myself in the stomach with a broken bottle. After that, my father put me in the cellar. He tied up my hands and beat me. That's when I was sent to the psychiatric hospital in Jury-lès-Metz for three months. I left home eight years ago. I haven't seen my father since, and I don't want to see him again.'

A grisly story, and I didn't know what to think of it. I hadn't imagined Heaulme as an abused child. Could this explain his impulses to kill? But was he telling us the truth? If not, when had he lied? Everything would have to be checked. Find his father, his sister, their neighbours at the time, the psychiatrists …

The purpose of the personal history is above all to encourage the accused to talk about himself. The less the judge intervenes, the better. The magistrate steered Francis Heaulme onto the subject of his schooling and work life.

'I often missed school because I was ill a lot. Very highly strung. I had to repeat the year several times in primary school. I don't remember the names of my teachers. I remember more about when I went to the Briey special school. I was sixteen. I trained to be an electrician, and I qualified. My father had told me that if I failed, I'd be sent to reform school in Château-Saint-Louis. But I didn't end up there because I passed my exams. At school, if anybody picked a fight with me, I gave them what for. I had quite a few warnings. I was often called up before the head. I was suspended sometimes. I didn't learn anything. When I was at Briey, I had an argument with the cook over a piece of chicken. I wanted to take the biggest bit. The cook didn't like that and we got into a fight.'

He was giving us his version of events, making up a qualification, and displaying the aggressiveness that seemed to have dogged him throughout his life. It was always somebody else's fault, mainly his father's. How long had he been this dangerous? We would have to trace the primary and secondary school teachers, and the employers, who had known him well.

Francis Heaulme was now very relaxed. He continued his story with complete detachment.

'At nineteen, I began to work with my father as an electrician for temp agencies in the Metz region. I was paid, but it was my father who pocketed the money. At twenty-one, I worked for the civil engineering firm Metz-Lorraine Travaux Publics. It's still going ... I worked with a very nice site manager ... I used to go hunting with him on Sundays. I didn't shoot, because I don't like that. I was the tracker. We hunted boar and roebuck. I remember that time very clearly and I have happy memories of it. I stayed with that firm for five or six years, but I was sacked because of alcohol. I didn't get on with the foreigners who worked with me.'

Francis Heaulme reeled off his story as if it were a recitation, the words chosen with care. Even when he had to talk about himself, he gave nothing away. Too much coherence in an account where everything tied up neatly ... and a wealth of detail – places, dates and people. In this respect, Heaulme had an outstanding memory ... I was now convinced that he was testing us.

'I lost my job and my mother almost at the same time, and that broke me. I ended up at the psychiatric centre in Jury-lès-Metz ... I wandered from Emmaüs community to Emmaüs community to find my niche. I still haven't found it ... I stayed at various different Emmaüs communities all over France. Metz, Haguenau, Dunkerque, Boulogne-sur-Mer, Caen, Cherbourg, Brest, La-Roche-sur-Yon, Rochefort, Nice, Bayonne, Montpellier, Pau, then I came back up to Bischwiller ... I only stayed two weeks at the community in Brest because of the discipline, it was like being in the army. I kept myself to myself, I didn't hang around with just anybody.'

After a few moments' silence, he added, suddenly agitated, 'I don't want to hear any more about the Emmaüs communities. I won't talk about the past any more!'

Heaulme clammed up. Possibly a new lead, but for the magistrate, this was not the moment to try and establish the truth. He was simply recording Heaulme's version of events. Impassive, he signalled to his clerk to start a new paragraph concerning Heaulme's military service.

'I was declared unfit for service because of my eyesight. I don't like uniforms. I was glad to be declared unfit because I don't like the army. I had enough discipline with my father, thank you.'

'Fine! What about your love life?'

'I've known girls, but it didn't work out because of my personality. I've got a foul personality. I'm stubborn. I'm very shy and sentimental. I can't remember the names of the women I've known. I was more involved with my work than with women. At weekends, I'd go to bars and meet women, but not prostitutes. More like women aged twenty-five to thirty-five, married or single, but I didn't go very far, I just chatted them up.'

Before Francis Heaulme's arrest, his girlfriend had described their meeting as a gift from God. 'The Almighty placed him on my path. I was cycling past where Francis was working as a labourer.' Afterwards, according to her, they were inseparable. With hindsight, I shuddered at the extreme vulnerability of this woman. Her blind trust could have proved fatal. Paradoxically, perhaps it protected her.

Francis had his own version of their relationship. 'I was never violent with her. Sometimes I shouted when we argued. I would go out to prevent things getting out of hand. With her, I feel happy. All alone, I can't cope.'

He had indeed settled down, but I was convinced that he was making up his sexuality. For what purpose? There was a sexual element in his attacks, but I couldn't yet put my finger on it.

'Tell me about your health, then your tangles with the law', the judge went on.

'I've never had a serious illness or operation. It was after my mother's death that I began to have a serious alcohol problem. I drank mainly beer and whisky, sometimes I mixed the two. I used to drink five to twelve litres a day. I saw military uniforms in my mind. I often ended up in psychiatric centres because of the drinking. When I'd had enough, I'd leave without any explanation. When I drink, I don't know where I am any more. I fall over. When I drink, I'm lost and I call my mother ... One of the doctors who looked after me told me that if I carried on drinking, things would end badly for me. I might finish up in hospital. I admit I used to be an alcoholic, but I'm not any more. I've completely changed my personality ... Around August or September 1989, I was sentenced by the Montluçon court to forty-five days in jail for mugging an elderly person. I stole 50 francs and I turned myself in to the police. I was released at the end of September. I spent a week in a hostel in Montluçon, but I don't remember which one. Then I had a train ticket to go home to Metz. In July 1989 I went to the gendarmerie in Compiègne-lès-Arcs to report that I'd been run over by a car, but it wasn't true. I never found out what the verdict was.'

Once again, he was on his guard. Both in Brest and Avignon, Heaulme had been hospitalised just before a murder. He was a regular patient. He knew exactly how medical establishments worked. He would always volunteer to lend a hand and do odd jobs, and was easily accepted by the nursing staff, who looked on his 'respite cure' with a charitable eye. It was a made-to-measure alibi.

Changing the subject, the judge asked about his leisure activities.

'I used to like getting on my bike and going for a ride. On Sunday evenings I'd go and see some friends at Bischwiller church. I don't know their names, but we got friendly ... We talked about God and about everything. I'm very religious, I say my prayers every night. I went swimming in Haguenau ... I used to spend a lot of my time at work.'

Lastly, the magistrate asked him the names of the people he could call on as character witnesses.

'I think the people from the nursing home at Château-Walck could talk about me ... They're friends. I can't think of anyone else who might talk about me other than those I've mentioned.'

'Fine, excellent ... I don't have any more questions. Is there anything you would like to add?'

'No, nothing.'

Francis Heaulme smiled. He was like someone who had just taken an oral exam and was pleased with his performance. He had given his version of his past. A 'clean' past with the worst parts airbrushed out. The presentable story that he wanted the judge to accept. But he had taken the precaution of slipping in a few extenuating circumstances: a violent father, an unhappy childhood, alcohol … But not a word about his victims, not a hint of remorse. He had been perfectly in command, from beginning to end of the hearing. It was an impressive display of self-control.

The judge reread the interview out loud, then they both signed the statement. The session was over. The judge ordered the defendant to be taken back to his cell.

Francis Heaulme rose slowly, thanked the magistrate and turned to the escort. The handcuffs went back on immediately. His counsel then told him that he would come and see him soon in prison. In the corridor, after a limp, evasive handshake, I spoke to Francis: 'I'll still be here tomorrow. I could come and see you if you like.'

His face relaxed and he replied, visibly pleased, 'Yes, come and see me. I'll be waiting for you.'

The next day, at 9 a.m., I was outside the gates of Brest prison – a modern building, less than ten years old. If it were not for the watchtowers and high grey concrete walls, it could almost be a student hall of residence with bars. Incarcerated here for about ten days so far, Francis Heaulme was not entitled to special treatment. He did however have a cell to himself. Contrary to the usual practice, he had not transited via the first floor of the prison, reserved for 'newcomers'. The prison administration feared the reaction of the other detainees. The Moulin Blanc murder had shocked everyone, even the local thugs. The minute Francis Heaulme had arrived, rumours of revenge started to fly.

After going through the double entrance doors, I crossed the little yard and waited outside the heavy door until a warder opened up and allowed me into the prison complex. A long beep, and the door swung open. I entered and soon found myself faced with another obstacle. This time, a metal gate. A second electronic buzzer and I was inside. A warder greeted me from behind his glass window. He then directed me using the remote surveillance system, like an air traffic controller. Another maze of corridors and doors, and I finally reached the investigators' tiny visiting room. Three chairs and a small table filled the entire space. I had barely arrived when Francis Heaulme was in front of me.

'Hello, Francis! How are you? I'm pleased to see you.'

I meant it. This time, there was no question of talking about the Brest murder. This meeting was outside the framework of the original investigation, so conditions were ideal for a relaxed discussion. I expected a 'lighter' conversation than our previous talks. On the other hand, I knew that he was capable of going off at all sorts of tangents, in particular of the most sordid kind. Nevertheless, I still hoped that he would at last explain to me the reason for his killings.

'I'm fine,' he answered, calmly. 'I've written to my sister. She's going to come and see me soon.'

He no longer wore his contorted facial mask. His attitude towards me had changed. I couldn't help feeling surprised.

'Francis, I'm not here because of what happened on the

beach, it's out of my hands. Now it's between the magistrate and you. But I need you to talk to me about your life, but not the way you did to the judge. By the way, why did you carry on like that?'

By asking that question, I hoped to get us back into the mood of the conversation we'd had in Strasbourg, when he described his crime with the utmost naturalness. I also wanted to show him that I hadn't been taken in by his games.

'I was afraid. I can't say everything. This business isn't my fault. When I was on the road, I was sick, you know that. Besides, wherever I go, there are killings.'

His face hardened and his eyes bored into mine.

'Francis, if you're sick, the experts will be able to see that, and if the right place for you is a hospital, that's where they'll send you. But you must talk. If you remember what happened, just tell the truth. Where shall we begin?'

I didn't want there to be a lull, and it was my turn to stare intently at him. I hoped for an immediate answer. He went on, 'Brest, was a cock-up, I told you. Besides, '89 was my black year.'

His tone was hard. What did he mean? The year he had committed the most murders? Was he trying to express remorse for the first time?

'OK, so '89 was a bad year for you, Francis, but why?'

'Because I left a witness that time. "The Gaul", it's his fault, it's his fault I'm here.'

I was flabbergasted. It wasn't remorse, but sheer exasperation for not having got rid of the witness to his crime! His black year was the year of anger. But I didn't turn a hair. Heaulme went on:

'You know François, before, I was sick, I used to think I was at war. It was because of the alcohol and the medicines. I was afraid. It's not my fault!'

He was going round in circles, but I was beginning to detect in his speech a way of protecting himself and preparing me for his version of events. It was never directly he who committed a murder. The protagonist with the strange dreams where death became reality was a sick alcoholic, dosed up with medication, abused by his father and mourning his mother. It was 'somebody else' who did these bad things. Not Francis.

'It's not my fault!' That sounded like a cry for help. He was misunderstood, imprisoned in his solitude since childhood. He had a desperate need to talk and be listened to. I sometimes felt that I had become his confidant. Because he knew that I didn't judge him and because he thought I really knew him.

'Listen, Francis, I'm ready to help you, but don't tell me any more fibs. Other police officers will be coming to interview you, do you know that? They might not think you're any different from other criminals. You risk life imprisonment. So tell me about yourself and the other person you were. Then I can point out the difference and everyone will understand.'

Francis Heaulme became serious again and his beady little eyes stared fixedly. He seemed to be racking his brains for some disconcerting reply.

'I've had a lot of cock-ups, François, but that's all in the past. I've changed. I don't want to talk about it any more.'

Now he was dodging the issue. I had to find another tactic, another way in.

'I'll tell you what, Francis, take this sheet of paper, if you like, and write down the "cock-ups" you remember now.'

He grabbed the sheet of paper, placed it in the centre of the table, picked up the pen and settled down to write. Then he looked up, a little nonplussed.

'What do I write? I don't know how.'

'Francis, just write down the names of the towns where you had a "cock-up". If you remember the date, put that down too. That's all. In any case, only write down the things you remember clearly. I'm not going to chase around after your fantasies if you remember the whole business clearly, OK?'

My reply made him smile.

'I'm not certain of all the dates, François.'

It was working. The blank page seemed to mesmerise him and force him to get the words out. Heaulme wrote like a primary school child, slowly and laboriously. He produced a list of dates and towns.

'On 2 January '86, I was at the Emmaüs community in Peltre. On 8 January in Haguenau. On 5 May in Metz, I worked with my father. I lived at my grandmother's. On 7 ? '86, Périgueux. 10 ? '87 Boulogne-sur-Mer. On 10 ? '87 Lille, cock-up. In '88 Metz. In May '89 Brest cock-up, '89 Reims, '89 Avignon, '89 and 90 Christmas day Auch, '89 Marseille and Courthézon cock-up, 10 ? '90 Metz, '91 Bischwiller.'

He looked as if he were writing with a pen of lead so heavy

that his hand could barely move. He put down the pen and handed me the sheet without a word.

'You see, Francis, it's easier to work like this. I'm going to go and see what happened in these towns, and when the investigators come and talk to you, they'll already know a bit about you. I'll talk to them about you. Did you write down everything, by the way?'

'No, there are others, but I need to think. It's all muddled up in my head, because of the medication.'

So he never stopped playing games. I refrained from asking the slightest question, but I was worried by all those names written on that quarter page. Thirteen towns. And just as many 'cock-ups'? I feared so.

'Francis, apart from the "cock-ups", can you tell me about the towns you liked?'

His memory suddenly came back to him, but this time, I was the one writing. Without pausing for breath, he listed thirty-five places, from Nice on the Riviera to Saint-Omer in the north. For each one, he gave the year he had been there. He was no longer talking about fantasies or confused memories. The tension had gone, we were talking normally. What a mug's game! I was convinced that he was still withholding something. What was he afraid of? Did he fear he would not be deemed insane if he remembered?

A warder knocked at the door of the visitors' room. It was lunchtime. Heaulme had to go back to his cell. He rose abruptly. 'Come back and see me again, François, we'll finish it next time. I'm going to think about it. Cheerio!'

Without looking round, he walked over to the waiting warder. I watched him disappear down the corridor.

As I got back into my car, I felt tired. I knew that I had taken another step forward, but this latest interview with Heaulme had exhausted me. Every second was full of tension. Not showing anything. Thinking about every word, every gesture. My eyes boring into his, so as not to break the tenuous contact. I felt as though I had raised a two-tonne weight from the seabed using a horsehair yarn.

He enjoyed our conversations, but only disclosed a few fragments to give me a glimpse of the extent of his crimes, which made me in a way a helpless bystander. He was placing me in a labyrinth peopled with dreams, fantasies and riddles. Only by solving these would I find my way out.

7

Inside the mind of the killer

For several days, messages piled up at the secretariat of the criminal investigation unit. With the agreement of the investigating magistrate, I passed on all the information about Francis Heaulme to the national gendarmerie. Each unit thus had the reconstituted itinerary of the murderer over three years. Requests for interviews came pouring in from all over the country. My superiors were thrilled.

Scanning through them one by one, Colonel F could barely conceal his satisfaction. His department was now in the limelight.

'There are now more than ten criminal investigation departments that want to interview him,' he said to me, putting down the documents.

His attitude towards me had changed. I had the feeling that he was aware he had gone a bit too far that day in July 1991 when, following the opinion of Major JR, he had refused to let me go and question 'The Gaul' in Bayonne.

'Abgrall,' he added, holding out the messages, 'talk to the judge and get permission for all these investigators to interview Heaulme. I'd also like you to inform these departments of the dates when they can come to Brest prison, OK?'

The content of these messages was impressive. All of the cases were serious, the murders particularly gruesome. But in some instances, it was hard to make the connection with Francis Heaulme. With the phone wedged between my ear and my left shoulder, a pen in the other hand, I called all the investigators concerned, one by one. This led to long conversations. Each one described his investigation. Our questions often overlapped, and I sensed the hope that this new lead was kindling in my colleagues.

The presiding magistrate and I agreed that, initially, only the investigators who had established that Francis Heaulme was in the vicinity of their crime would be invited to question him. These measures were to avoid confusion. I eventually managed to draw up a reasonable schedule. There would not be more than two departments pursuing their cases at any one time.

Two weeks later, the authorisations were ready. As instructed by the judge, Reims and Bordeaux would be the first two criminal investigation units to be permitted to come to Brest prison. The memory of my last visit was still fresh in my mind. The warder had interrupted us too soon. Francis Heaulme had taken advantage to slip away quickly. I had the hunch that he would have liked to continue the conversation. So I decided to see him one last time in private, before the arrival of my colleagues. Was he even aware of what lay at the root of the violence that possessed him? As for his itinerary, his memories were so clear that there was no room for lies. He recalled perfectly where he had been. But who had he really met? And to what extent were his murder fantasies real? I wanted this game to be over.

Once again I stepped inside that oppressive world where one set of doors only opens after another has closed. I made my way to the visiting room.

'Go in and sit down,' said a warder, noting down the time of my arrival in his register. 'I'll call the prisoner's floor. They'll bring him down.'

It was 1.30 p.m., and this time we had a bit of time before us. I decided to sit in the same room as before. The table was still as small, but how can I describe the walls, which were a dull, sad yellow, covered with grimy handprints. It made the place even less hospitable.

A few minutes went by. Gradually, the sound of doors opening and closing grew louder. He was coming. Then he was in the room, standing in front of me.

'Hello, François, you came back,' he said, looking me straight in the eye.

By now I was accustomed to his using my middle name. His curt speech was not aggressive. It was just his way of communicating, that was all. I rose and held out my hand. He responded, as embarrassed as ever, almost forcing himself.

'How are you, Francis?'

'All right,' he said, very stiffly.

Then, abruptly changing the subject, still standing in the middle of the room, he blurted out:

'One day I saw a woman on a patch of waste ground. She was dead. I don't know where. That was in 1989.'

He stood still and watched me. He had just picked up the thread of the conversation at exactly the point where we'd stopped at our last meeting. It was barely believable, as though his thoughts had been frozen since. With all the calm I could muster, I invited Heaulme to sit down.

'I'm listening, Francis.'

His hard face betrayed no emotion. And yet I could sense that he wanted to talk. I took out the little piece of paper on which he had noted down the towns of his 'cock-ups'. And we were back at exactly the point where we'd left off, two weeks earlier.

'I saw a fellow grab a woman. He punched her and kicked her. It was dark. The "other" chap spoke German. He was wearing fatigues. I couldn't do anything. Then a farmer arrived on his tractor, and the police came. I was hidden. After that, I left.'

'Where was this, Francis?'

'I can't remember. It was after Brest.'

So it was after May 1989. We stared fixedly at each other. The 'other' again, that protective double who made the unacceptable palatable. He knew I had understood. So why was he still talking in this way? I said nothing. He continued:

'In 1990, I saw a murder on Route de Vallières. A gippo,

Jean-Marie W, was stabbed twelve times in the back by an Arab. He threw his knife down by the body.'

It was essential not to ask any questions. I knew nothing of these crimes. Were they real? A Gypsy, an Arab … What did he mean? Were they his victims? Accomplices? Perhaps, but I didn't think he could have acted with an accomplice, that wasn't his style.

'Francis, were you stopped by the police or the gendarmes at any time after that?'

'Yes,' he replied, 'but I gave my other names — Pascal Nagel, Francis Herman, François Picard, Francis Marchal.'

I listened to him and stated calmly, 'I know all that, Francis.'

He was surprised at my reply, and seemed relieved. In actual fact, I couldn't believe my ears. I needed a break. I felt that he was opening up. These affairs were murders, I was convinced. I hadn't imagined that he would use aliases, but how far had he gone? Suddenly, he burst out:

'A long time ago, on a Sunday, I was cycling down a street. It was in eastern France. There were some houses on the left. On the right there was an embankment and a railway line. Two kids threw stones at me when I rode past. At the end of the street there was a stop sign, a bridge and some dustbins. I left. When I came back later, I saw the kids' dead bodies near some railway carriages. There were also police and some firemen.'

Did he murder those children? I couldn't bring myself to believe it. It was horrifying. 1989, his 'black year', when he'd made the mistake of leaving 'The Gaul' alive … What year was he talking of now? He carried on telling his stories, without emotion. His painfully stilted speech made listening to his allegations even more excruciating.

'In Marseille there's a little square, you go down some steps and there's a fountain. There I was mugged by a fellow with a knife. He wanted to take my bag. I fought back. He was a foreign backpacker. I ended up in hospital. Another time, in Auch, on Christmas night, behind the church, I had an argument with a beggar. He was on a seat. I hit him with his stick.'

I had no idea what else he might have to tell me, but for the time being I wanted to leave things there. If these statements were true, they were too important to be recorded in this manner. I needed to think clearly and review all this information. I didn't have the time to say anything, he persisted relentlessly.

'In 1987, in Metz, I was walking around near the Porte des Allemands. I saw an Arab being stabbed in the back by skinheads. They knifed him three times. He was walking his dog. And he had his slippers on.'

I wondered whether he was aware of the significance of his words, or whether he was expecting a reaction from me.

'In Bayonne, in 1990, I had a really good time. I was at the Emmaüs community. There were cliffs,' he went on. 'One afternoon, I went to see the sea. There was a girl with a bicycle on the cliff top. I went down to the water's edge. When I got to the bottom of the cliff, she'd jumped. She was lying dead on the rocks.'

How long could he carry on talking like this? What was all this really about? It was time to bring this interview to a close.

'Francis, it's good that you're telling me about your travels, but you're not telling me anything new. I think it would be best for you to tell all this to the investigators who are coming to question you. The whole of France wants to hear what you have to say. I'll be back soon to introduce them to you.'

No use, he couldn't hear me.

'In 1990 I went to Spain, to the Emmaüs community in Pamplona. To Belgium too, to Namur. And to Germany, to Berlin. Will they be coming too?' he asked without a trace of irony.

'I don't know yet. In any case, we'll have plenty of time to talk about it all, Francis.'

I tried once again to stop him.

'Francis, I have to go, I've got an urgent meeting. Do you need anything?' I asked, getting to my feet.

'No, François, I've got a TV. Goodbye!'

Behind this icy energy, I could sense he was both amused by this situation and rather glad to have talked. In the depths of his shining eyes, I even discerned a certain pride. He brusquely rose and went to the door. Next to the heavy blue door was an outsize window, a blend of architectural modernism and prison functionalism ... I walked over to join him. Through the window I gave a little sign to the warder. He smiled and the door opened. Francis was accompanied back to his cell, without so much as a backward glance. It was 2.30 p.m. I had only been there an hour, but I felt as if I had run a marathon. I was dazed by what I had just heard.

The minute I left the prison, I went straight to the Law Courts. The second floor was where the examining magistrates' offices were. I raced up the stairs and soon found myself in the judge's chambers. I met his clerk in the corridor, and she invited me in. Sitting at his desk, the judge waved at me.

'Good afternoon, Mr Abgrall. Come and sit down. Here, I've prepared your authorisation to contact other departments. If the investigators can't come on these dates, don't worry, I'll change them without your having to make another appointment,' he said, handing me the pink forms.

'Thank you, Your Honour. But I need to talk to you. Do you have a moment?'

'Go ahead.'

'I've just come from the prison, where I met Francis Heaulme. On my previous visit, we talked about his itinerary and he mentioned his "cock-ups". I thought he would carry on in this vein and that we would piece together his travels. Instead, he listed a series of incidents that he supposedly witnessed. I'm afraid these may be new murders. Now, the way he presented things, his behaviour ... everything suggests that we may be dealing with somebody who is mentally ill. In any case, I find it hard to work him out. He's disturbing.'

'But what exactly did he tell you?' asked the judge, intrigued.

I went over my surreal conversation with Francis Heaulme point by point. It only took a few minutes to see the effect of his words. The magistrate thought for a moment. Eventually, he replied:

'Listen, I think you should launch some fresh investigations. It is essential to find out whether these incidents took place. Personally, I'm not in charge of these cases and cannot do anything on my own initiative. I think it is too soon to infer anything, but if the facts confirm what he's told you, talk to the public prosecutor. As to his insanity, I have just received the psychiatrists' and psychologists' reports. In all likelihood, Francis Heaulme will not be deemed "irresponsible". He will be brought before the court in Quimper. Here, look!' The magistrate showed me the two reports sitting on his desk. 'You may read them, if you wish.'

I nodded. He handed me the files.

In criminal cases, the defendant undergoes two examinations. One, the psychiatric examination, is to determine whether the accused was insane at the time of the crime and whether he or she is suffering from mental illness. The other is a psychologist's report to assess how dangerous the individual is. The experts have a number of elements to draw on, including police statements relevant to the case, hospital records, an interview with the defendant and psychological tests.

The first report began with a letter from a psychiatrist who had treated Heaulme for several years.

Mr Heaulme was an in-patient at Jury-lès-Metz psychiatric hospital on thirteen occasions from 1982. He has always

119

presented a psychopathic tendency and finds it hard to cope with
the constraints of institutional life. He frequently requests various
forms of assistance, but has failed in everything he has
undertaken as soon as it has been presented to him in the form of
a contract.

Already, all the ambiguities of Heaulme's character were evident. What was he seeking in disclosing his problems but refusing help?

He also seemed to react very strongly to frustration. He was violent with the other patients, but aware of this violence, which never seemed to the doctor to be of a 'sexual nature'.

That was Francis Heaulme, all right. And yet his tragic action on the beach must have opened up a new avenue of exploration for the psychiatrist.

We examined Mr Francis Heaulme almost three years after the
event. This is a very long gap, allowing every imaginable
reconstruction in a subject who has been a frequent patient in
psychiatric hospitals, which has made him conversant with
psychiatric culture.

Was this preamble the customary reservation or did it imply that Heaulme's character was especially difficult to pin down? Did he make up answers? On the next page, Francis Heaulme presented himself succinctly to the expert. It was the same story as usual, except for one detail. He had taken on his father's profession. He stated he was an industrial electrician.

He is articulate when he·wishes to be, his speech is a little stilted, he finds it hard to express what he wants to say, and he makes up for this by gesticulating when he talks. He easily gets bogged down in details.

Were they really details?

His language difficulties reveal his educational shortcomings. It should be added that as a child he spoke both patois and French. He presents as someone of average intelligence. From the start, he stressed the violence of his father, whom he has not seen for several years. For him, effectively, this is the explanation for 'this whole business that he's being blamed for'.

Of average intelligence ... It was certain that Heaulme was not the innocent he sometimes pretended to be. There was no doubt about it, he was definitely the killer. There had to be something that incited him to murder. The rest was a long biography during which Francis Heaulme retraced the milestones in his life. His violent father, the death of his mother, when his world fell apart, being on the road, alcohol ... I knew it all by heart, more or less.

In 1986, Mr Heaulme decided to leave. '1986, that's when I ...', meaning that since then, he has led an itinerant existence, wandering from hostel to hostel, getting himself thrown out on a regular basis for alcohol abuse. He is unable to give precise details of his travels.

Why in 1986?

In Saint-Lô, he was arrested by the police. During questioning, he said 'that he had been in the commandos, that he liked to kill and he added that he had not been detained.' He left for Caen, then Metz and Blainville. There, having lost his ID documents, he went to the police station, where he knew he was wanted. 'Wherever I go, there's a murder. I was accused of a murder near Avignon.' Once again, he added that he was allowed to go free.

'Wherever I go, there's a murder ...' What audacity! Had Francis duped the psychiatrist? Nothing seemed to bother him.

An attentive subject, he seeks to explain himself and convince, telling us, by the way, that he was waiting to be able to talk to the experts to get them to understand what had happened to him ... He is fully in command and at no point in the conversation did he show any emotion. There was no rise in his pulse rate or blood pressure by the end of the examination.

Did he always manage to remain so cold? He really was imperturbable.

The expert then focused on the cause of his many scars. He examined Francis Heaulme's arms and torso, and noted:

If he harmed himself sometimes, it was never during the real periods of depression, but much more during bouts of

*drunkenness causing psychomotor arousal. 'That's how I am, I
explode,' said Francis Heaulme.*

The following analysis explored the subject's emotional side.

*He sometimes experienced a sense of unease, a feeling that he
had not been understood, not been heard, that he had nobody to
confide in, that he was seeking happiness without being able to
define the object of his search. This reflects a certain
dissatisfaction with his life, an unrequited emotional search much
more than a depressive state or neurotic tendencies.*

Could that lead to murder?

*There is no indication of progressive or overt mental illness. Some
police statements give the impression that Heaulme has a very clear
recollection of what happened during the murders. The allegation
of fantasies, dreams or fictitious scenarios that became reality but
had nothing to do with him do not correspond to any psychological
model for which there might be a scientific explanation.*

He was not mentally ill – I found that hard to believe. On the
other hand, his fantasies always corresponded to an actual
murder. The following analysis reinforced my own impressions.

*Heaulme cannot be considered as presenting a dangerous state in
the psychiatric sense of the word. On the other hand, it seems to
us that he presents a dangerous state in the criminological sense of*

the word. If he is the author of the crimes of which he is accused,
we have not encountered any indications that permit us to state
that, at the times of the crimes, he was in a deranged state as
defined by Article 64 of the penal code.

In other words, Heaulme was conscious of and responsible for
his actions. In the everyday sense of the word, he was not 'mad'.
He would have to stand trial.

Heaulme also took the Rorschach test. The object of this
exercise is to reveal a person's level of aggression. In these well-
known tests where the subject is asked to interpret famous sym-
metrical inkblots, some people see butterflies, or flowers,
depending on their personality.

Francis Heaulme was unable to control his speech, and his
interpretations of the blots were coloured by violence and
morbidity. 'Two people having an argument ... No, who are
fighting ... There are red spots ... It's blood ... There, I
squeeze him with my hands, he howls like an animal, there's
blood everywhere ... I squeeze, I can't help it.' Then, without
any transition or particular affection, Mr Heaulme reverted to
very standard interpretations, devoid of any emotion.

I found these last lines perturbing. Despite this new insight
into the murderer's personality, a number of questions remained
unanswered. His sexuality had barely been touched on, whereas
I was still convinced that his crimes were of a sexual nature.
Francis Heaulme continued to remain an enigma.

Back at the unit, I had a meeting with Colonel F. He quickly grasped the situation, and reacted promptly. 'Start a preliminary national computer search, try and identify anything that matches his statements. Meanwhile, I'll contact the police crime division HQ. If you have any problems, my office is at your disposal.'

Every indication of his unconditional support ...

The next morning, I invaded the unit secretary's office. To her great despair, I had brought all the files with me. This was where our computers were. Sitting at the terminal, I did a search using keywords that would enable me to identify the cases that interested us. The locations, modus operandi, the years and the names given by Francis Heaulme — all these details were transmitted to the central computer.

After nearly an hour's wait, the results came through; they were indisputable. No case was a direct parallel with the declarations made by the Moulin Blanc murderer. I was surprised. There must have been problems with cross-referencing the files. I input the data again, adding a few variants. The results were identical. Neither murders nor assaults. It was unbelievable. When I told Colonel F, he decided to call Rosny-sous-Bois — the nerve centre of the entire gendarme force — in person. I waited in my office.

A quarter of an hour later, the telephone rang. It was my superior. In a voice that brooked no interruption, he asked me to come to his office. As I neared the door, I reckoned that this time, it was over. I was going to be told to stop investigating Heaulme and to go back to my other cases ... and for the time being, I was at a loss for anything to say.

8

A trail of blood

Against my expectations, the Colonel had called me in to assure me of his support. He was well aware that our database had surprising limitations. On this occasion, we realised that cases dealt with by the police department were not necessarily logged on the computers of the gendarmerie, especially in the case of old crimes. It was a sizeable loss of information. Furthermore, without an exact date, a computer search often proved fruitless. So I fell back on traditional methods, the telex and the telephone. One by one, I called my colleagues in Marseille, Strasbourg, Bordeaux, Paris and elsewhere, on the trail of Heaulme's 'cock-ups'.

Thus I collected a set of data that more or less corresponded to the incidents described by Francis Heaulme, like the following episode in Auch, for example. The local police recalled clearly that there had been a knife fight between two vagrants behind the church one Christmas night, but there were no records of the proceedings. In any case, on 23 and 28 December 1990, Francis Heaulme had been treated at the city's hospital for an injury to his forehead. Was it a simple spat between drifters?

And that attempted theft near a fountain in Marseille which he claimed to have been a victim of ... The local gendarmerie confirmed that Francis Heaulme had indeed been admitted to the Becker hospital following an assault. Now, that same day, 6 August 1989, a foreign hitch-hiker had been admitted to casualty at the same hospital. 'Stomach injury inflicted by a bladed weapon', read the report by the fire officers who had brought him in. Registered under a false name, this man had vanished as soon as he was able to get out of bed. A mere coincidence? An argument that got out of hand again? Or that simmering violence of Francis Heaulme's that could boil over at the slightest provocation?

And what to make of the assault, Route de Vallières in Metz in 1990, which Heaulme claimed to have witnessed? The gypsy he claimed to have seen killed in a fight with a North African really had died. Except that, on the day of the crime, Francis Heaulme was in Quimperlé, 850 kilometres away ... Not to mention the fact that this crime had not taken place on Route de Vallières as he had stated. What did it mean, what message had he been trying to convey?

In Bayonne, during the summer of 1990, the body of a girl had indeed been found at the foot of a cliff. The initial investigation had concluded it was a suicide. At the time, Francis Heaulme had been staying in the local Emmaüs community.

Even more surprising, on 8 August 1990 the Biarritz-Plage fire brigade was called out to assist a man who claimed to have fallen from a cliff. This was a Charles Francis, one of Francis Heaulme's aliases. These facts were sufficiently worrying for the investigation to be reopened.

And then there were the children found dead beside a railway line. There was no record of them in any file. Try as I might to fathom the man, this time I had no key to understanding him. These cases remained elusive, but I did not discount my hunch that Heaulme could have been behind them all. He made nothing up. The psychologist's report emphasised his involvement in the scenarios he described, but to what extent it was impossible to tell.

On reflection, I could only see one explanation, and that was that each scenario Heaulme described was made up of several true-life incidents. But he mixed up the dates, places and people so that it was impossible to link them with any actual cases. If that were true, he had us well duped. I had to probe further.

It was no accident that he had managed to slip through the net for so long, nor was it luck. He had a system in place, but how did it work? I didn't know yet, but the answer was perhaps in the places where he had said he'd had a 'cock-up'. They probably had some significance for him, but what was it? It was a pity I couldn't go and visit these places, I was convinced that seeing these different sites would provide new clues.

As for his aliases, research into these yielded astonishing results. The names he chose were not random. There was a logic to everything. This much was now clear. He used the name of a neighbour from Metz, his grandmother's maiden name, that of a vagrant he had stayed with in Cherbourg. Only the name Herman did not seem to have any connections … Unless it was that 'other' who spoke German and whom Francis Heaulme had seen '*grab a woman in a field and punch and kick her*'.

Again, the Reims investigators had alerted me to this attack. Heaulme's account was very similar to one of their cases. They were coming to Brest that week and wanted to meet me.

Late morning on 23 September 1992, the commander of the Reims unit arrived, accompanied by a major. When they got out of their unmarked car, I was surprised to see that they were in uniform. They were impeccably turned out and their military air gave no hint that they had just driven more than 700 kilometres. The look they gave the barracks spoke volumes. It was true that the old, grey building near a major road intersection was rather unprepossessing, even when the sun was shining. It was even more depressing than the Law Courts. The introductions were brief and courteous.

'Will you be available for the duration of our stay?' inquired the officer.

'Absolutely. I'm at your service.'

My reply brought a smile to his lips. We were both keen to get down to work. I suggested going straight to the Petty Officers' Club where rooms had been booked for them. This military hotel in the city centre is very useful for visiting officers. Furthermore, it was a pleasant place.

The dazzling white seven-storey building housed several treasures. It also had a stunning view. From their windows, the commander and the major could contemplate the whole of Brest harbour. They were delighted, and this made contact between us all the easier. They settled in, and at lunchtime we met in the large restaurant. Our table was slightly apart from the others.

'If you don't mind,' began the officer, 'I'll tell you about our investigation over lunch, and, of course, why we are interested in Francis Heaulme.'

So, without asking any questions, he gave a detailed account of the investigation into the death of a thirty-year-old woman who had been found naked in a field one morning in July 1989. I listened attentively. At times the major broke in and added certain details. They knew the case inside out. I could see that this new lead had raised their hopes, but their speech remained cautious. They were both experienced investigators, and they knew only too well how a new avenue can very quickly turn out to be a dead end. The way they let me in on their investigations, including their failures, showed the trust they placed in me. We were aware of the special bond that exists between investigators who handle these difficult cases. They had been working on this one for more than three years. I knew what an investment that represented. Our food had been served and was already cold. The commander apologised.

'I wasn't aware of the time passing. So do you think Francis Heaulme could be involved?'

They needed to appreciate the complexity of his character for themselves.

'I suggest that first of all I describe to you his behaviour when he was held for questioning, and then when I went to see him in prison. But first of all, I think you'd find it useful to get acquainted with the Moulin Blanc case. If you like, we can visit the scene of the murder. I'd rather proceed in this way so that you can form your own opinions more easily. You may find that there are similarities between the two cases.'

They seemed satisfied with my reply. Outside, the sky had suddenly turned cloudy. At 2 p.m., as we stepped onto the shingle of Moulin Blanc beach, it started to pour with rain and there was a strong wind. We walked towards the Sables Rouges headland, passing two fishermen on foot, curious to see us inspecting the scene. Our attitude must have given away our purpose.

'You know,' said the commander, 'this is an extraordinary place to commit a murder. You can be seen from anywhere. The same applies to our case, in fact.'

Being back there made me feel uncomfortable. Storms had slightly altered the contours of the beach, but the main locations were still identifiable. I gave them details of the crime scene, showing them the precise spots where the photos in the file had been taken, walking across the shingle as the murderer had done on that day in May 1989.

My colleagues did not say a word. They were absorbing the atmosphere of the place as I had done three years earlier. Having finished our inspection of the beach, we decided to go back. Before returning to the gendarmerie, we drove past the Emmaüs community where Heaulme had stayed. I pointed out the other access to the beach, the path the murderer had used.

On our arrival, the criminal investigation boss invited us into his office for a coffee. The Aline Pérès dossier lay ready on a table for them to consult. The major then handed me part of their file. It was my turn to examine their findings. It was too late to look into three years of inquiries, so I concentrated on the scene of the murder and the immediate surroundings. As I turned over the pages of photographs one by one, I noted that there were striking similarities between this new crime scene and the ones with which I was familiar. Another murder near a road. The unusual violence of the killing. The sexual aspect of the attack. And the victim, someone quite ordinary. It was all there.

'Is there anything you need to know?' asked the major.

'No, well ... Could you hand me the autopsy report?'

Reading this document was just as revealing ...

5.30 p.m. We had finished reading through each other's documentation. Now it was time to prepare for the interview.

'If you're ready,' I began, 'I'll describe to you my experiences of interviewing Francis Heaulme.'

Everyone stopped talking. Sitting round two desks, François and my new colleagues listened. I slowly launched into my account, but after a few minutes, they started firing questions. The officer began, 'You say he can talk normally, without bringing in fabrications or other actual experiences, so why does he keep doing this with you?'

'That's what intrigues me. I am convinced he's playing a game. He's protecting himself by mixing up different incidents. In fact, he never makes anything up, but he transposes the different stories, even if, paradoxically, he's taking a risk. But for the time being, nobody has been able to identify these cases. He is perfectly aware of this. I also believe he likes to dominate, to feel that his interlocutor is powerless in the face of his stories. The worst thing is to think that in talking about them, he is in a way reliving his acts. This behaviour is consistent with the psychiatric reports. Until now, he has only spoken clearly to me once. We were having lunch, in Strasbourg. That shows he pays attention to the context; as far as he was concerned, he was no longer in custody. Remember he is mentally lucid and knows perfectly well what we are driving at. He remembers exactly what he did, and what he said. Above all, don't ask him any questions to which you don't have the answer. Let him talk.'

I sensed that they were receptive to my advice.

'How can we manage that, if all we have are suspicions that he may have been involved in our case? This fellow's going to take us for a ride. It's impossible to know everything about his movements ...'

'You've seen how long he's been on the road,' the major went on.

'That's precisely the situation I found myself in the other day in the prison. He blurted out a whole series of stories when I'd asked for nothing, and I decided to cut it short as fast as possible. In your shoes, I wouldn't ask him anything other than where and when he stayed in Reims. If he went there, he'll tell you. You'll be amazed at his memory.'

The officer spoke again.

'Perhaps you'll be able to help us during the interview?'

'Francis Heaulme knows me now. He notices everything. If we hesitate over a question, or exchange glances, for example, he'll sense it. I'll try and get him to relax in your presence, then you take the lead. If you feel that one of his answers eludes you, don't go back over it. It's better to stop the interview and check what he says.'

'But,' said the major, 'if he talks to us about somebody else instead, we won't know whether it's true or not. We'll have to mention it in the interview and he'll see exactly where we are at.'

Then I remembered Francis's behaviour in Strasbourg.

'In the Brest case he spoke to me about "another" man who had stabbed the victim. That was when I asked him to do me a drawing of the beach and what he had seen. He was very precise and positioned all those involved. Quite simply, by the time he had finished the drawing, the "other" had turned into himself. There was no make-believe character any more. What's more, the interview had continued without this "other" man being mentioned again. A sketch of the scene is probably the solution.'

The questions stopped there. We were all secretly wondering how the interview would go.

'By the way, I nearly forgot to mention that it would be better if you came to the prison tomorrow in plain clothes. Francis Heaulme told me that uniforms make him want to kill.'

My two colleagues exchanged dubious glances.

'Who on earth is this character?' muttered the major.

We returned to our hotel.

Next day, at 2 p.m., the three of us were outside the prison gates. After checking our IDs, the warder opened the heavy metal door into this other world. We walked in silence, each mulling over the questions he wanted to ask.

As we neared the visiting rooms, I broke the silence.

'If I introduce you to Francis as acquaintances, I'll have to use your first names, is that all right with you?'

My question amused them.

'No problem. I'm André,' replied the commander.

'And I'm Claude,' added the major.

A warder came to meet us.

'Are there three of you?' he asked in surprise. 'We're going to have to find some more chairs if you all want to sit down.'

We found another couple of chairs in the room next door and seated ourselves in the little visiting room, the same one as usual. I was beginning to feel at home there. Claude took out his typewriter while André seemed to be concentrating his mind.

'If you're ready, I'll have the prisoner brought in,' said the warder.

To avoid surprising Francis, I waited for him by the entrance to the visiting rooms. A few moments later, his tall frame appeared behind the metal grille. The door opened, and in two strides he was facing me. Behind his fixed smile, I thought I could detect that he was pleased to see me.

'Hello, François, how are you?'

This was the first time he had asked after me.

'Fine, Francis, and what about you?'

Our hands brushed. He did not reply. He had spotted my colleagues in the visiting room.

'Come in, Francis, and I'll introduce you. Meet Claude and André. They do the same job as me, and they have a few things they want to ask you.'

Francis Heaulme stared insistently at them and avoided shaking hands. He was already very tense.

'Go on, sit where you like.'

I sat down beside him. André was the first to speak.

'We're from Reims, and we'd like to talk about your travels on the road.'

Claude was still busy preparing forms. Heaulme looked at me obstinately.

'I told you there were some other people who wanted to meet you, and here they are,' I said.

My words diverted his attention away from me. His gimlet eyes lighted on André. He gazed fixedly at him, giving the impression that he was trying to read his thoughts. Of his own accord, he began the slow account of his endless travels, interspersed with war scenarios, citing one by one the towns he had passed through. He told an anecdote or made a comment on each place, as if he wanted to prove that he had really been there. We listened closely while Claude busied himself at his typewriter. Francis Heaulme had been speaking for an hour, when abruptly he stopped. For a few seconds, the only sound was the clatter of the typewriter keys. What was going on? Heaulme seemed to have run out of steam. He looked from one of us to the other. This claustrophobic little room had not been designed for spending long periods of time in, especially when there were four people. It was hot and stuffy. Claude took off his sweater. Heaulme went on:

'Actually, I've got good memories of Reims.'

Then he gave the dates, described the buildings, estimated the distances between different points in the city, and eventually told us how he had witnessed the killing of a woman on a patch of waste land, giving full details.

Francis Heaulme was now ignoring me and speaking directly to Claude. He probably knew that nobody believed his version, but he continued with astonishing aplomb. The 'other' entered the scene.

Claude immediately handed him a sheet of paper and a pen, and asked if he could do a sketch to describe the incident. Francis drew his chair up to the little table, like a schoolboy. Hunched over the paper, without hesitation he drew a map of extraordinary accuracy, using only a section of the page. We watched him in silence. This sketch made Francis Heaulme the number one witness.

The 'other' had disappeared. The tension was almost tangible. Francis finished and handed over his drawing, which he dated and signed. André spoke:

'We're going to stop now. I think we'll be back in a few days.'

Taken aback, Francis Heaulme looked at me. I said nothing. As usual, he rose without a word and left the visiting room with the warder.

A few minutes later, we were back at Brest gendarmerie. Claude did not disguise his satisfaction.

'As soon as we've checked Francis Heaulme's statement back in Reims, he'll be charged. His sketch definitely corresponds to the scene of the murder. The rest is less reliable.'

These were the words of an investigator sensing that the end was within reach. I understood him, but I couldn't help thinking about the missing material. The many details of the murder Heaulme had witnessed ... A different case in all likelihood. My two colleagues decided to leave the next morning. They needed to review the case with the investigating magistrate as quickly as possible in the light of this new evidence.

We returned to the Petty Officers' Club. André and Claude invited me to dinner. As soon as I walked into the hotel restaurant at 8 p.m., André said:

'Talk to me about anything you like except murder, OK?'

'OK, but only if you buy me a drink.'

After this light-hearted beginning, it turned out to be a short evening. The session with Heaulme had been exhausting, confined as we had been in that tiny prison room. At 9.30, we retired to our rooms.

The next morning, I accompanied my two colleagues to their car outside the ancient grey gendarmerie building. Just before driving off, André said:

'We'll check everything out and then we'll be back.'

No sooner had they left the premises than a colleague called down to me from the window:

'Your boss is on the phone, quick!'

The colonel wasn't the sort who called his staff for nothing. Something must have happened and a team needed backup. I rushed up to his office.

'Hello, Abgrall, have you still got your two rooms booked? Then hold on to them. The Bordeaux unit is arriving tomorrow. Jacky R and an investigator from Périgueux are coming to question Heaulme. The magistrate has given his authorisation.'

Things were beginning to move fast. The case they were working on wasn't classed as a priority. Even if their dossier had all the hallmarks of the Moulin Blanc killer, there was one significant detail that continued to worry me. The murder they were investigating had been committed by several people. For the moment, there was no indication that Francis Heaulme had been involved, even less with an accomplice.

A few hours later, the Bordeaux investigators arrived. Their dossier also contained a horror story. On 9 May 1986, the battered body of a young conscript doing his military service had been discovered in a gym in the centre of Périgueux. Laurent Bureau was twenty years old. His killers' footprints could be seen in the pools of congealed blood.

The case had been removed from the police department originally in charge of the investigation as a result of serious procedural errors. Two vagrants had been imprisoned and subsequently cleared. The file, somewhat depleted, had landed on Jacky R's desk four years later. These were not ideal working conditions, but on listening to these investigators and seeing their determination, I realised that they might have something.

They too were experienced. The details of the Moulin Blanc murder and the profile of the killer I outlined did not deter them. On the contrary, they pinpointed a number of analogies with their case.

The presence of an accomplice ... Perhaps that was the question Francis Heaulme was waiting for me to ask? If that was the case, I thought that Laurent Bureau's name could be added to the list.

It was 9.30 a.m. when we entered the jail. The chief warder was getting used to my visits.

'You again, Jean-François, come to see your friend?' he asked, adding, 'In here he's as meek as a lamb, you know ...'

'Don't you believe it, Jean-Yves,' I replied with the utmost seriousness. I knew only too well how dangerous Francis Heaulme was beneath his quiet façade.

Once we'd agreed on using first names, Jacky R placed his laptop on the little table. He had prepared a list of questions the day before. Christian sat next to him.

I gave them one last word of advice:

'Be low-key, show that you want something from him, but look him right in the eye. He likes to dominate the conversation. He'll talk.'

As soon as I caught sight of Francis in the corridor, I knew something was amiss. His face was closed, he did not look happy to see us. He greeted me curtly. I barely had time to reply before he was in the room.

'You're here about Charleville, you're here about Charleville-Mézières!' he insisted, addressing Jacky.

'Not at all, Francis, they're from Bordeaux, not Charleville-Mézières.'

'I thought they were here about Charleville-Mézières. So, you're from Bordeaux?'

At once his face relaxed. He changed his tune, no longer displaying the animosity he'd shown on assuming my colleagues were from Charleville-Mézières. He was interested. A new game was about to begin for him.

'That's right, Bordeaux,' Jacky reassured him.

Heaulme sat down and immediately launched into an account of his travels, adding some new twists. He clearly seemed pleased that I was there. I was certain he had mentioned Charleville-Mézières on purpose. He was playing games. When he included little changes in his life story, he glanced in my direction. There was no longer any scorn or contempt, he was seeking my connivance. He was pleased that I didn't contradict him. Actually, he was using the situation to send me messages. Jacky asked:

'I have a photo album to show you. It has pictures of people you might have met on the road. Would you look at it?'

Heaulme leaned over the table and slowly studied each photo.

'I met this bearded chap in Charleville-Mézières. At the time I was wearing a short-sleeved shirt and velvet shorts … He told me that he and some others were living in a squat. He invited me to stay … To get to the house, we walked two or three kilometres … We arrived around 10 o'clock. Then some other people came. A Turk who I only remember vaguely, a very fat German, aged around thirty-five. He didn't speak French.

There was also an Arab with a blonde woman aged about thirty to forty. She had a dachshund on a lead ...'

Christian broke in and asked if Francis could do a sketch showing the location of this squat. Wordlessly, Heaulme obliged with his usual precision, once again providing a wealth of detail. He even mentioned the colour of the shutters. Jacky said:

'But you've just drawn the outskirts of Périgueux, not Charleville-Mézières!'

Francis turned to me in fury. He could not cope with being confronted with his contradictions.

'I'm going to smash the place to bits! I'm going to smash the place to bits!' he shouted.

But from his expression, I could see that he was still in control. In fact, that message had been addressed to me. It was his way of asking me if he could. He didn't want to lose face.

'Do what you like, Francis, but don't touch the computer, it's mine.'

He had to get out of this situation so that we could resume our conversation. It was time for him to know that I wasn't necessarily against him, that I wasn't trying to judge him, but simply to understand why he had killed. Christian and Jacky were baffled and were on their guard.

Heaulme suddenly leaped up and violently overturned his chair. My colleagues immediately restrained him. He didn't touch the computer. I had what I wanted. In asking for my permission before acting, he had just revealed a chink: he needed someone. My attitude also suggested the possibility of a closer relationship.

Christian asked him to sit down again and threatened to handcuff him. Heaulme slowly obeyed. He was extremely tense. As he lowered himself into the chair, he shot me a grateful look. He had just let me know that he trusted me. I was beginning to read him. At his recent interviews, he had placed me in the position of powerless witness to his violence, akin to that of 'The Gaul' on the beach. Now at last I was going to be able to change that role.

After Heaulme's outburst, Jacky decided to suspend the interview. On the way back, I could sense that my colleagues had doubts about me.

'I imagine you didn't like me telling Francis Heaulme to do as he pleased?'

Before I could say any more, Christian interrupted. 'No we didn't. Supposing he'd picked up the chair and smashed the computer.'

Then I told them what I thought had really been going on during that scene. I insisted on the fact that it revealed a weakness in Heaulme. Eventually, they agreed with my analysis.

The next day, we all went back to our own units. In the light of these recent developments, Colonel F contacted the police investigation bureau at the gendarmerie HQ. There was a strong likelihood that a joint unit would be set up.

The cases were still a long way from being resolved, and Francis Heaulme had now been incarcerated for nearly a year.

Two months later, on 7 December 1992, my colleagues from Reims were back in Brest. We were ready for them. Over the last few days, we had exchanged several telephone calls. They had drawn up their list of questions. We met at the prison. I found the little room very useful. Not changing rooms has its advantages. People aren't distracted trying to acquaint themselves with new surroundings, they already have their bearings and are better able to concentrate from the start.

Once again, we were there not to accuse Francis Heaulme, but to request information from him. Until now, that was the only method that had ever worked.

When Francis Heaulme entered the room, we were ready. He looked at me and I knew at once that this time he would not be playing games. He sat down. André and Claude asked their questions, to which he replied in minute detail, intricately describing elements that were sometimes of little importance. He still had a pensive air. He was probably thinking of another incident. Three hours went by, less fraught than usual.

Francis Heaulme concluded his interview with a rapid gesture. He hastily signed the pages, as if to rid himself of a problem. While André and Claude gathered up their documents, I walked out into the corridor with Francis.

'Is something the matter today, Francis?'

'I'm waiting for the ones from Bordeaux,' he replied.

His tone was ironic, and I could detect his impatience. I was certain that he had already prepared his story, gone over and over each morbid detail as he brooded in his cell. Shut away from the world, he could no longer destroy others now, but he had found compensation in something that seemed to give him enormous pleasure, which was sending investigators chasing around on the trail of his crimes. Was this a means, typical of Heaulme, of continuing to torment his victims?

André and Claude were satisfied, they had their suspect. They had found the session easier and Francis Heaulme less intimidating than anticipated. This was true, and there was every indication that he had lost interest in the Reims case. Everything had been said on the subject and so he could no longer derive any pleasure from it. For him, there was no more challenge. He had moved on to something else. To another murder.

Meanwhile, in Périgueux, Jacky and Christian had done a colossal amount of work and had identified one by one the Turk, the German, the North African, the blonde woman and two other witnesses. So it was all true. The itinerary Francis Heaulme had outlined had led them to an attic room. It was time for another interview.

'We've questioned the bearded fellow Heaulme mentioned,' Jacky announced on arrival. 'He confirms that he met him in Périgueux.'

This time, it was clear that our suspect had not always acted alone. We were going to have to widen our field of investigation.

The next day, back at the prison, Francis seemed eager to see us.

'I thought you were coming earlier,' he said, loping into the room.

Then he inquired after my colleagues' health, expressing con-

9

The trail continues

Colonel F, walking ahead of me, pushed open the glass door of the forensic research centre of Rosny-sous-Bois HQ. He went over to reception and introduced himself and me to the officer on duty. Today, after several months' wait, we had an appointment with several members of the senior command of the gendarmerie.

We crossed a spacious lobby and descended the staircase leading to the basement rooms. On the way, I met a number of acquaintances. The building is a real meeting place, where investigators from all over France bump into each other in the pursuit of their inquiries. There are fewer than 400 of us and eventually we all come to know each other.

We entered a long, narrow room, with no windows or heating. It was February 1993, and a little warmth would have been welcome. Six people were already seated at tables in a board-

cern that they might be tired after such a long journey. This thoughtfulness was most unusual for him. We remained on our guard. He sat down and Jacky began the interview.

'We have a lot of questions to ask you. When you arrived in Périgueux, which establishments did you contact?'

Francis replied willingly, but his answer soon took a chilling turn.

'Actually, when I arrived at the hostel, the fellow with the beard asked me what I was doing that evening. As I had no plans, he invited me to go with him to the park, next to the hostel. There, we waited for some other people. The fellow with the beard had brought some wine. The Arab, the woman and the Turks joined us. We sat down near the statues. The one in photo number three joined us about an hour later. He was drunk and aggressive. He tried to provoke me by asking what I was doing there. Not long after that, he called over to a young man who was crossing the park on his own. He was carrying a travel bag. He seemed to know him. He grabbed his collar and demanded his money. The young man didn't want to hand over his money and the other fellow head-butted him.'

I stopped him:

'The "other" fellow?'

He smiled and picked up again immediately, his eyes riveted on Jacky, as if to convince him.

'That's when I stepped in. I separated them. I told him to leave the kid alone. The young man, definitely a soldier, fell on the ground. The other fellow kicked him. He was unconscious. The Turk and the Arab took the soldier's clothes off. We just stood and watched. They picked him up and carried him out of the park.'

Christian couldn't help darting me a look. Francis Heaulme continued to put forward his version of events, as always without a trace of emotion. His description of the gym where the young man's body was found was extremely accurate. I watched him. He wasn't merely recounting the scene, he was back on the basketball court again, reliving it.

'They put him on a big mat. I was hidden in a corner of the room ... His hands were tied behind his back. It was the Arab who took the fire extinguisher off the wall and passed it to number three ... There was blood all over the floor ...'

It was gruelling, as it always is when a murderer confesses. But this time, we had to remain composed and continue to act normally as if what we were hearing was perfectly natural. It was important not to snap the tenuous thread that connected him to us.

Jacky brought the session to a close. It had lasted five hours.

Francis Heaulme went back to his cell wearier than usual. For him too, these sessions were draining. It is exhausting trying to be constantly in control. This time, he looked wiped out, as if he had come back from a very long journey.

Christian shared his first impressions.

'The mat, the hands tied behind the back, the fire extinguisher, it was all there, but it's a hell of a muddle. I still don't know which of them were really in the gym. We've got a lot more work to do ...'

Périgueux, Reims, Avignon and Brest: four charges already.

For a long time I had thought that the Moulin Blanc murder the work of a lone killer. In a way, I wasn't completely wro Heaulme had nearly always lived alone and rejected by eve body. These latest cases pointed to new possibilities. Heauln did not have a particular type of victim. They could be young old, tall or short, fair or dark. They could be men or women but always people who were vulnerable. The scenarios h dreamed up and ended by acting out were fluid. Another aspect of his psychology was emerging. He liked to surround himself with an audience when the opportunity arose. Minor roles, like 'The Gaul', which Francis Heaulme set up like pawns and made reluctant witnesses, but who could very well become actors in the crime if he so decided.

As it happened, in the Bordeaux case, Francis Heaulme's accomplice, charged at the same time as him, was called Didier G. Another vagrant whose name was to become tragically famous. He was found guilty of another murder: that of a seven-year-old girl, killed on the banks of the river running through the village of La Motte-du-Caire. It is awful to think that fate brought together these two men driven by the same killer urge I feared that there were more of Francis Heaulme's accomplic at large, but how many? Could they too be serial killers?

room arrangement, facing each other. An officer from the senior command, the commander of the technical department and his divisional heads introduced themselves in turn. We sat down and took out our notebooks. The senior officer spoke first.

'As you know, we are here to set up a joint unit to investigate the criminal activities of Francis Heaulme. The criminal investigation units of Rennes, Bordeaux and Reims have alerted us to the need to open fresh investigations, as this man may have committed other murders. That is why I have brought you together. You represent all the gendarmerie's investigation units.'

He turned to me and asked, 'Abgrall, you who have a particular relationship with this man, how would you set up the investigation?'

I hadn't expected to be put on the spot like that. I had thought there would be several proposals, but it seemed it was up to me to suggest the way forward. I mustered my thoughts and went ahead.

'Francis Heaulme has been on the road since 1984. He is currently suspected of four murders between 1986 and 1989, all in different towns. Consequently, we need to find out where he stayed and what happened in those places.'

'Is it possible?' the officer asked the commander of the technical department.

'Probably,' he replied.

'You just need to draft a new notice about this man and circulate it to all units,' added a divisional head, 'specifically requesting the dates and towns where he was stopped for an ID check.'

But we all knew that these requests were sometimes shelved even before the whole department had seen them. I jumped at the opportunity.

'It is essential, without going any further, to centralise the replies, even the negative ones, so as to be certain that inquiries have been conducted in every town.'

By lunchtime, everything seemed settled. With Colonel F's authorisation, I was to be sent on secondment to Paris, to the national gendarmerie headquarters. A joint unit was set up to coordinate activities at national level and liaise between the investigators.

I was officially in charge of this unit. A message was sent out to all the gendarmeries up and down the country and a liaison officer was appointed in each criminal investigation unit. If need be, this officer would assist me. At Rosny-sous-Bois, a data-processing expert would provide me with support, especially in identifying cases likely to be relevant.

These were considerable measures. This time, the senior command was providing serious resources. Given the numerous trips I was going to have to make, I was even given a car-hire budget and in exceptional circumstances I was permitted to fly, which was unheard of.

After a brief lunch, we set off back to Rennes. There was heavy traffic on the Paris ring road. Taking advantage of the opportunity to talk, Colonel F turned to me and said, 'Things are moving forward, Abgrall, you're going to be able to get on with the job now. You know, I've never seen a position like yours within the gendarmerie. The decisions taken today were unprecedented. It's an opportunity, I'm sure, but there are also risks attached to the job. There are no free radicals in the gendarmerie, just remember that.'

He was right, and on reflection I felt this warning was probably useful. The other designated personnel remained attached to their units, except me. I was, in a way, suspended in the void. If I ran into difficulties, there was no guarantee that this freedom that I was enjoying wouldn't turn to my disadvantage. But there was no question of doing a U-turn.

'Thank you. I'll try to bear that in mind.'

A week later, I was back in the belly of the fort of Rosny-sous-Bois, attending a meeting with the head of the Assault and Battery division. He showed me into a tiny room near his department.

'You'll be able to work in peace here. Don't worry about the photocopier, it doesn't work, so nobody has any reason to come here.'

The fort suffered from a dire shortage of space, so being allocated a room the size of a large cupboard was considered fortunate. The chief added, 'Stay there if you like, I'll go and get your new partner.'

I preferred to go with him. In a neighbouring office, he introduced Christophe, a slim man aged around thirty with a discreet air. He had been at the meeting with the senior command, and knew what it was all about.

While the introductions were being made over coffee, I quickly realised that he was thrilled to be involved in this investigation.

'You know, here it's always the same old routine. A question from one unit, a search, a reply and you start all over again. In your case, there are cross-references to be made, and I'm going to centralise everything. It's a different ball game.'

I was in luck. This man was methodical and sharp to boot. He had given some thought to the question of computer cross-referencing the cases and had come up with some solutions.

We soon set to work. His office was barely big enough for two people, but we made do as best we could.

As I listed the points I wanted to include on the identification sheet, we talked about Francis Heaulme's personality. Christophe took notes, identified key dates and asked me questions.

By 4 p.m., we had finished. The identification sheet read as follows:

Francis Heaulme has probably committed a number of murders all over the country. Does not always use the same method (bludgeoning to death, using a weapon – a rock or knife, strangulation with external injuries). Does not appear to use a firearm. Chooses his victims at random and leaves them naked or partially naked. Has probably committed double murders. Gets himself sent to hospital.

Information is required on evidence of his passage (hotels, hostels, particularly Emmaüs communities, police reports, police station log books and psychiatric hospital records ...), unsolved

murders, missing persons and discoveries of bodies, applications to
various public services, social welfare offices, town halls, fire
services (transport), hostels, hospitals ... The period we are
interested in is from 1 January 1984 to 8 January 1992.
Information to be sent to the technical department at Rosny-
sous-Bois with the code name 'Heaulme Francis'. These checks
must be completed by the end of April 1993.

We included six photos of the murderer. They had been
taken between 1989 and 1992. Heaulme's expression changed
dramatically from one year to the next. The one from 1989, for
example, with its grimacing, tormented look, was particularly
disturbing. On the other hand, in the most recent one, dated
1992, Francis, with short, neatly combed hair, looked calm.
Potential witnesses who had met him during this period would
have seen one of these two faces.

Christophe then programmed the central computer. In a few
seconds, our request for information had been sent out to some
fifty regional gendarmeries and police stations.

Throughout the period in question, Heaulme had been continually on the move. There was a strong likelihood that he had
left numerous traces. We didn't expect to have to wait long for
the replies to start coming in.

The second phase of our computer search was less certain. It
was a matter of identifying all the unsolved murders carried out
in similar fashion to those we had already recorded. We would
then be able to classify them in order of priority, and attempt to
link them.

I said to Christophe, 'Try over the last ten years, from 1981 to the end of 1991. Anything prior to that is invalid.'★

'That far back?' asked Christophe in surprise.

'Yes, absolutely. The murders we know he committed show considerable expertise. He must have begun his career very early.'

Christophe set to work.

'OK, but I have no idea how many this is likely to throw up.'

One by one, Christophe typed in the codes corresponding to the crime categories. Each offence, each crime had a letter and a number. After a few minutes of this tedious task, he pressed 'Send'. All we had to do was wait. Five minutes went by. Suddenly, the phone rang. My partner picked it up. 'Yes, yes, speaking ... Yes, I've just sent it out ... What? 1,125 cases! ... OK, OK ...'

Christophe replaced the receiver.

'Christ! Did you hear? Apparently I nearly jammed the whole system. If we want to process your question, we have to do it at night, when nobody's using the computers. I'm on duty tomorrow evening, I can do it then.'

1,125 unsolved murder cases in only ten years! I had predicted less than a quarter of that number. I was way out. I was in for some sleepless nights ...

★ Translators note: In France, after a period of ten years from the closure of the investigation, no further investigations can be carried out, even if the criminal is subsequently identified.

While waiting for all this data to be gathered, I decided to visit the various units that might be able to help me. My first stop was Reims. Francis Heaulme had been charged and transferred to Reims prison for questioning.

The Reims gendarmerie barracks are at the end of Rue Robespierre, just opposite the prison – so close that gendarmes and prisoners are almost able to talk to each other from the windows. Both buildings date back to the nineteenth century. High red stone walls conceal these drab edifices where the monotony is only relieved by the tricolour flag. By comparison, the Brest garrison wasn't so rundown after all. Francis Heaulme was just a stone's throw from my new residence. This nearness would make my life easier.

After the customary greetings and a quick lunch, Claude informed me that Francis Heaulme, told of my imminent visit, had been asking to see me for days.

With a few strides, I was at the prison gate. Under the gaze of a surveillance camera, I rang the buzzer and introduced myself. A good five minutes ticked by before the little hatch in the forbidding steel door opened. A face appeared, and looked left and right. 'Are you alone?' I was asked. I replied that I was and could not repress a smile. The hatch was closed and the jangling of a heavy bunch of keys announced my entrance. I had the strange feeling of stepping back in time.

The contrast with Brest was striking. Much smaller, this three-storey prison was built of solid stone. The broad, thick walls gave a foretaste of the design of the cells. Square rooms, slightly oppressive, with little rectangular windows positioned too high to see out.

I crossed the yard. I only had to go through two metal gates before reaching the visiting room. The narrow room was like a sort of stall, with barely room for two chairs and a table. Not only had the environment changed, but the space in which our meetings took place was also smaller.

Francis Heaulme soon arrived. He was wearing his perpetual purple tracksuit which he had been wearing on the day of his arrest. He opened the conversation immediately, as if he had been waiting for me for a long time.

'Ah, François, you came. It's not as nice here as in Brest; there are foreigners and rapists. I don't like that, but it's easier for my sister. It's not so far, we'll be able to see each other more often. She said that a famous Paris lawyer is going to defend me for free.'

Then, in a confidential tone, like a child who is afraid of having done something wrong, he added, 'You know, I didn't tell the fellows from Bordeaux everything. In the gym, it was me who tied up the kid's hands. I took the lace from my shorts. I grabbed his two hands, but it was too short, it didn't hold. The lace stayed on his right wrist.'

This was too much. I didn't want to get caught up in his game of half-truths again.

'Stop, Francis! I've had enough of your play-acting. I know who you are. You had more than enough time in Brest to tell them all that. Talk normally and stop this, otherwise I'm going. Why did you want to see me?'

Heaulme was taken aback and seemed flustered. For a

moment, he appeared to withdraw into himself. Disappointed at having made me angry, he almost apologised.

'Just tell them to come back. I'll explain to them. You know, I don't always remember everything. I used to drink, and with my medication, I would sometimes have fits.'

Maybe, but I didn't believe him. I told him so.

'Fine, that's understandable. You should have said so. But I don't think that's everything.'

Now he was staring at me coldly. I went on.

'Are you afraid people will find out what you did? Well that's what's going to happen. It would be better if it came from you rather than from the investigators.'

He was worried.

'I know you know,' he said, as he had done three years earlier. 'But I'm not a sadist, François! I'm not a sadist!'

He added, raising his voice, 'I've forgotten what I did. I don't want to talk about it any more. I told you, I was another man, I was sick. I used to drink. That's all.'

At no point did he ever express, or even feel, any remorse for his deeds. I could see that he was distraught and there was no use pressing the point. In truth, I feared he never would, and that I would have to probe further, deep inside him, to find each fragment of his lethal make-up.

I resumed the conversation on a lighter note.

'Is there anything you need here? Clothes?'

'No, they offered me some, but I prefer my own … The TV's free. The governor came to see me. He told me I could call him if I had any problems.'

'He's a nice governor … Are you alone in your cell? Do you get out a bit?'

'I'm alone. I prefer it. Here there are kids who've killed old people, that's nasty. I'd better not come face to face with them … so I don't go out for exercise any more. I don't like the types who are there. I keep to myself.'

'And is everything OK with the warders?'

He answered with a laugh, 'They call me Mr Heaulme, like a governor.'

I smiled.

'That's impressive! … Francis, I'm just opposite, at the gendarmerie. I have to look after the investigators who will be coming to interview you. So if you could talk to them in a normal manner, that would be good. You can tell them anything, they're used to it. Anyway, it's up to you … If you need to see me, let me know. Now I'm going to have to leave you.'

He looked at me closely. He seemed sorry to see me go. I rose. He asked me:

'Did you come from Rennes to see me? Are you going back there today?'

'Yes, I've come from Rennes, but not just to see you. I've also got things to do here.'

'Come back before you leave.'

We went our separate ways. His friendly attitude towards me left me perplexed, but I was still mindful of who he was and, above all, what he was capable of doing. There was no question of my taking his side. He was a killer, I was a cop. It was the only reasonable attitude possible. What's more, he had stopped playing games when I'd asked him to ... Next time perhaps he would unburden himself freely.

A little later, back at the Reims gendarmerie, I received a message from Christophe. He had a case that might be of interest to me.

On 7 May 1991, the body of a fourteen-year-old girl, Laurence Guillaume, had been found in a field at Servigny-lès-Sainte-Barbe near Metz. Another naked female body, abandoned in a field not far from a road.

I was two hours from Metz. I decided to go there the next morning.

On my arrival, the reception I received from the homicide team was rather frosty. They couldn't understand why I wanted to poke my nose into their business. Their case was the only homicide in hand.

The most sceptical was my contact at the station, Pedro. In his forties, with chestnut hair, light-coloured eyes and a headstrong air, the only thing that was Mediterranean about this native of Metz was his surname, which was why his colleagues had nicknamed him Pedro ... He did not believe for one moment that this case had anything to do with Francis Heaulme. He stated that he had checked Heaulme's movements, and he was in the clear. Even better, he claimed he had identified young Laurence's murderer, and that he was a local man.

In front of the assembled crew, who were polite but only half listening, I explained the purpose of my secondment and launched once again into a description of Francis Heaulme's behaviour. The indifference of Pedro and his team was blatant. As a matter of fact, they were only there because they were under orders from HQ. It was not a good start.

Even so, I wanted them to listen to me. Francis Heaulme was born in Metz: that was their patch! I pressed on. 'Route de Vallières, does that ring a bell? A gypsy knifed to death?'

Pedro glanced at his superior. After a brief silence, he replied, 'Route de Vallières? That's the road Laurence Guillaume rode down on her scooter. Just before she was snatched.'

He stopped short. From his expression, I gathered he did not intend to elaborate.

'Oh! By the way, I did respond to all your requests for information on Heaulme. If you want to read my notes, they're on my desk. You can use it this afternoon, I shan't be here.'

End of conversation.

After lunch, I sat down at a proper desk with enough space, at last. A fleeting little pleasure. It was nearly a year since I had set foot in Rennes, my home base. Pedro's office reminded me of my own.

The dossier compiled by my colleague was not devoid of interest. Between 1981 and 1987, Francis Heaulme had crisscrossed the region many times. I was particularly surprised at the number of spells in hospital, no less than eighty in five years, both in regional hospital centres and psychiatric hospitals!

I did not intend to stay there long. I would study these notes back at Rosny-sous-Bois. Meanwhile, I had to consult the impressive proceedings relating to the murder of young Laurence. The documents were methodically classified, but I would never get through them unless I made a drastic selection. Luckily, Pedro had created a computer index.

What had Francis Heaulme been doing that day? I switched on the computer ... There, Heaulme had been stopped by the police.

The two-page report dated 24/01/92 stated:

On 8 January 1992, we learned from the Strasbourg criminal investigation unit that Francis Heaulme had been arrested for murder ... The suspect being originally from Metz, we checked his movements during the period from 7 to 9 May 1991 ...

I carried on. Several people had been contacted by telephone, the nuns at the hostel where he had stayed, the managers of the rehabilitation association that had tried to find him a job, the members of a presbytery where he ate ... According to their evidence, he had been in Alsace at the time of the murder. Had I got it completely wrong?

On closer examination, however, I noticed that the dates given contradicted those of his stays in hospital which I had in front of me. I was taken aback. Visibly, the gendarmes were mistaken, but the report ended:

The investigations carried out have established that there is no link between Francis Heaulme and the Laurence Guillaume case.

I couldn't believe it. How could they have reached these conclusions without checking up on the spot?

I had to go back to square one. I put away these documents and took out the reports made after the discovery of the girl's body. The sheets of photographs were complete, and were accompanied by a map of the site. It was perfect. After examining them for two hours, I no longer had any doubts. The similarities to the other cases were too striking to be coincidental. The extreme violence of the killing, thirteen well-aimed knife wounds. Obvious expertise, as in Brest. The killer was in control of his victim: there were no marks on the body. No bruises or bumps. The murderer had not needed to stun or tie up the girl. There were tyre marks found near the body, but Heaulme couldn't drive. So he had at least one accomplice ...

I shut down the computer and put away the files. When Pedro came back at the end of the afternoon, I decided not to say anything to him. He wasn't the sort to take advice from a stranger, and he was pursuing another line of inquiry. Besides, I had nothing concrete. I asked him to show me the scene of the crime anyway, to which he consented unenthusiastically.

The next morning, I suggested to Pedro that we retrace Laurence Guillaume's route on the day of her murder. We set out from the centre of Metz. Pedro then began the detailed account of the fourteen-year-old's last hours, minute by minute.

'This is the site of the May Fair, a huge fairground. Laurence parked her scooter near the entrance, and chatted to some school friends. She had to be home by 9 p.m. She rode off down this street on your left. Route de Vallières, there it is. It leads directly to her house in Servigny-lès-Sainte-Barbe.'

'OK. There's one thing that is still bothering me. How do you explain the fact that Francis Heaulme talked to me about it?'

He didn't answer. I didn't press the matter. While he drove, I soaked up the atmosphere.

Everything happened within a radius of ten kilometres from Metz, to the east of the city. Servigny, where the girl had been kidnapped ... Vigy, the finding of the body and the clothes ... You needed a good knowledge of the area to get to these two villages at night. It is far from being a straightforward journey between the two. There are a number of intersections. The killers were definitely local.

The murderers had clearly tried to suggest they had fled via the Nancy motorway to the south of Metz. The victim's jacket, with her identity card, left as a decoy in a visible place in a petrol station, did not deceive anybody. The little road behind this station runs back into Metz. A childish strategy in stark contrast to the sophisticated kidnapping and murder.

I had mixed feelings about these contradictions. This disconcerting logic could be Heaulme's, but the Metz investigators categorically rejected this theory. Their behaviour seemed blinkered. I sometimes felt as though I had to spend my time convincing my colleagues how dangerous Heaulme was. In France, however, there weren't enough crimes of this nature to be able to brush aside the Heaulme possibility so lightly. And each time we found a similar murder, he just happened to have been in the area.

I went back to Rosny-sous-Bois. During my absence, a considerable amount of information had accumulated. There were details of 234 precise locations where Francis Heaulme had been logged between March 1984 and December 1992.

At the same time, we had whittled the initial 1,125 unsolved murders down to 94. We would have to sift through these, classify them in order of priority and contact the investigators. This took us several weeks.

A call from Claude made me think again.

'I had a visit from Pedro, from Metz. He went through my case file. He went and checked up on Francis Heaulme's movements. It turns out the Metz team had got it wrong. Pedro's thinking of coming to interview him on 16 June. We're expecting you.'

On the appointed date, Pedro was in Reims, accompanied by his partner. In the little meeting room, we made the introductions. The unit commander turned to the Metz investigators and said, 'You're going to meet a rather unusual character. The words "cock-up" and "accident" are code for murder, and "young people" for children. When he says he's not a sadist, it means there's been a violent sex attack. Make a note of everything he says, it might be useful to us. Any questions?'

Icily, Pedro replied, 'No … I'd like to tell you something. There was indeed an error in the report on his movements, but that doesn't make him a suspect in our case. We have another line of investigation. But we'll play along and note everything he says, even if it seems incoherent.'

Claude, escorted by a second gendarme, went to fetch Francis from the prison. It was so close that they went on foot. So as not to inhibit the Metz team, I would not be present during the interview.

A few moments later, Francis Heaulme was there, handcuffed. He was concentrated, slightly edgy.

'Ah, François! Where are the gendarmes from Metz?'

'They're here. I've told them what you saw by the Route de Vallières. I'm going to leave you with them. You'll tell them all about it yourself. We'll see each other after the interview.'

While talking, I walked with him into the room where Pedro was waiting. On entering, Heaulme asked him, 'Are you from Metz? That's where I'm from, it's good to see someone from home.'

I looked at Pedro, it was over to him.

Claude joined them. I vanished next door. I could hear just as well as if I were in the room. Pedro's tone was resolutely direct, and Francis Heaulme replied in the same manner. Very quickly, he started recalling his memories, his fantasies.

'I remember one day, in 1984 or 1985, I was working on a building site in Vallières ... I was with a kid who was working for the same company ... He was called Mustapha Mohamed, nicknamed "Le Moustache" ... I noticed there were ambulances and police cars around the Sonacotra hostel.* I went closer and

---

* Translator's note: Hostels/social housing where immigrant workers live.

I saw a man lying face down. There was blood on his back, his shirt was bloodstained. I asked an onlooker what had happened. He told me there'd been a stabbing. The next day, in the newspaper *Le Républicain lorrain*, I read about what I'd seen the day before, it was true ... The victim was a gypsy from Metz ... As far as I'm concerned, when I arrived at the scene, he was dead. I saw the ambulance men put him in a plastic body bag.'

It clearly wasn't possible. He hadn't been there on the day of the gypsy's death. What was the significance of this new version? It was even more detailed, and this time, he mentioned another man, Mustapha. There was no connection. He was embroidering. Why? Probably a character from a different scenario ... and the stabbing, the blood on the victim's back, the bloodstained shirt ... was he alluding to the murder of Laurence Guillaume? That was my belief. He thought he was manipulating Pedro, but he was giving himself away. Suddenly, he changed the subject. 'To help you in your work, I remember a murder case ... I was thirteen. A man nicknamed "Bouboule", who lived in Rozérieulles, was found dead in the stream with his head crushed ... I've always thought it was a murder, and the killer was Marchal ...'

What on earth was he talking about? Marchal was one of his assumed names! Pedro returned to his case, and again Francis replied dutifully.

'As I've already told you, I know the area well. Besides, when I was twenty-six, I belonged to a cycling club ... I cycled all around the Metz region ... Servigny-lès-Sainte-Barbe ... Ennery ... Pont-à-Mousson ...'

I traced his travels on a map and the connection became clear. Ennery was one kilometre from the spot where Laurence Guillaume's body had been found. It was the access road to the motorway where her clothes were discovered. He knew Servigny and the little road where the petrol station was. Pedro did not pick him up on it. He continued his direct line of questioning. Francis Heaulme had no difficulty following suit.

'... I heard about the Laurence murder on the television. I was at my girlfriend's house ... We watched the 8 o'clock news. I heard that a fourteen-year-old girl had been strangled in Metz ... Actually, it happened in Buchy, a village near Sainte-Barbe ...'

Pedro spurred him on, leaving no space for those little gaps between words that were so laden with significance. He was going too fast. Heaulme went on:

'... The girl was coming back from the May fair on her moped, that evening ... They talked about the father, who found the moped ... It seemed the girl had been followed by a car – a BMW, according to eyewitness accounts from neighbours in the village of Buchy – after she left the fair ...'

After several seconds' silence, he added, 'I had nothing to do with the murder of the girl called Laurence.'

The interview ended without Francis Heaulme and I being able to meet. He was taken back to prison. My colleagues and I exchanged our impressions of the interview. Pedro began:

'It will be difficult to go any further with him. He talked about the case because he'd seen the news. His allusions to the dead gypsy prove nothing. He's sick, he talks nonsense.'

Claude however was more reserved.

'We need to make further inquiries,' he said.

I backed him up.

'Heaulme showed that he knew the scene. I don't think we should stop there. We know he's never straightforward. Next time, ask him to do a detailed sketch. I think that for him, today was a sort of introduction, a review. He'll think about it and the next session will be very different.'

Pedro left frustrated, but agreed to a second meeting. This took place a month later, once again in Reims. The atmosphere was heavy with resentment. Pedro thought he was wasting his time. He still did not believe that Francis Heaulme could be the murderer. However, the interview still went ahead. Again, I was not in the room.

Heaulme spoke. 'I insist on being direct with you. On 7 May 1991, I knew that the May fair was on in Metz. I took the train on the Friday evening from Bischwiller. It was 4 p.m.... . I can't remember what time I arrived in Metz ... I met a fellow. Then, around 9 p.m., this fellow said to me, "We're going to get laid."'

Pedro broke in, 'What was this man like? Describe him to me ...'

'His name was Dominique. I met him in a bar ... He was about thirty, well-built, with a long nose and a scar on his right cheek ... He must have been about one metre eighty tall ... He had a little moustache. Most of his head was bald, but he had

shoulder-length hair growing from the sides and back of his head
… He was dark and violent … I even had a fight with him …
during one of my hospital stays …'

I was sure that most of these details had nothing to do with
the murder of young Laurence Guillaume. Francis was trying to
find out whether my colleague was able to identify this man
without him. He was protecting himself. Pedro reacted by
asking him to do a drawing.

'I can do you a sketch. I'll show you where I saw Laurence for
the first time with her moped … I can also give details of how
she was dressed …'

This time, it all added up. This was a good start. Pedro tried
to extract more information, but Heaulme realised that the
investigator was probing and jibbed. He replied slowly, giving
inadequate descriptions. The hours went by thus, without
yielding any further results. It was 2.30 p.m. when it was time
for the first break. I went into the investigators' room while
Francis Heaulme stayed in the room where a sandwich was
brought to him.

Pedro arrived, all fired up.

'It's him, I'm sure it's him!' he said excitedly.

His partner was an old hand from the criminal investigation
unit. He said, 'Stay calm, be patient, this is only the start of your
interview. You've got plenty of time.'

Then I suggested, 'Ask him to describe what "the other
fellow" who was with him did. I think he'll talk to you.'

Before the interview continued, I went to see Francis.

'How's it going?'

'François, they're from Metz, I'm happy to talk to them,' he replied, relaxed.

'Well, carry on, I'll see you later.'

He was on good form and not the least bit anxious. At 4 p.m. the interview resumed. The questions and answers were becoming increasingly lengthy, and increasingly muddled.

Heaulme was getting tired and my colleague was growing impatient. The hours dragged slowly by. I was beginning to find it tedious too. Then came a new version.

'... From now on, everything I tell you will be the truth ... When I arrived at the bar, I accidentally bumped into a young man who was with his girlfriend ... whose name was Laurence ... I apologised and offered to buy him a drink ... We had a drink together. Shortly after that, the girl, Laurence, said to the young man I'd bumped into, "I've got to go home now, my father wants me back by 9 o'clock." I immediately thought he must be a relative of Laurence's ... He said to me, "We'll follow her." He had a white Renault 5 ...'

Then he gave a detailed account of the kidnapping that had taken place that night. It happened around 11 p.m.

'She (Laurence) was wearing a white sweater, denim trousers and low shoes with little heels ... when she left, we followed right behind ... She went over the bridge beside the fair and stopped at the first red light ... she rode off again, past Le Gouest hospital, then past the petrol pumps just before the second traffic lights on the right ... she went straight ahead, then turned right at the fork in the direction of the cemetery ... After following her for a while, about fifteen or sixteen kilometres,

Dominique accelerated and hit the back of the moped with the right front bumper of his car ... The moped fell onto the verge and the girl was thrown off and lay on her back ... Before getting out of the car, Dominique asked me to take the torch out of the glove compartment ... I saw the rectangular yellow metal torch ... Then I saw there was a flick knife too ... I got out of the vehicle and went over to the girl, who was a metre away from the car ... she was lying on her back ... When she saw me, she swore at me ... she took off her helmet, and that's when I slapped her ... Dominique asked me to help him get her into the back of the car ... I refused and he put her there himself ...'

Pedro asked, 'And then what did you do?'

Once again, Heaulme gave a detailed account of the assault. He blamed the murder on his accomplice, Dominique. Pedro asked:

'You say it was Dominique who committed the murder, but you know as well as I do that your accomplice's name wasn't Dominique and that everything you have told me about the man you were with that evening is untrue, don't you? Well?'

Heaulme would not back down, but he knew that this time there was no getting out of it. He finally blurted out:

'I was desperate, I was wound up by everything that had happened. I took out my knife, an Opinel, not a flick knife, and I stabbed Laurence ...'

That was it. It was over. Heaulme had just admitted his involvement in the murder. The following questions merely clarified a few details. Pedro's tone had changed. Beneath his undisguised delight, there was already a hint of contempt for

Heaulme, which I didn't like. Particularly as three hours earlier he had been cursing about wasting his time.

Before returning to Metz, Pedro came to say goodbye. He told me who Heaulme's accomplice had been. 'The young man with him was Michel, the victim's cousin, he has a white Renault 5. You were right. I'll keep you posted.'

It mattered little to me that Pedro had changed his mind. I was still worried. Francis Heaulme had left me with the feeling that he was still playing games with us. Admittedly he had informed on his accomplice, but at the price of several months' work. He hadn't changed, he still wanted to dominate us. It was probably his *raison d'être*. With this new case, there was a whole new side of his personality to be explored. I was eager to meet his accomplice. What kind of man would be ready to follow someone like Francis Heaulme in his deadly madness?

10

Fear of the precipice

I did not in fact get to meet Michel, young Laurence Guillaume's cousin and Francis Heaulme's accomplice on the fatal night. Without formally opposing the idea, Pedro arranged things so that I was not present during the interview. I was merely allowed to see the transcript that was read out in court. Even on paper, it was harrowing.

My brother and I went around the fair. We had a drink, maybe two or three. At one point, this man came up to us and we chatted. We didn't know him, but he invited us for a drink. I remember he bought one or two rounds. I think Laurence had a drink with us ... A little later, Laurence told us she was going home. I asked her if she wanted me to light up the road with my

car headlights ... Then the man asked if he could come too. We
followed her in my light grey Renault 5. We drove 50 metres
behind her...

The young man then identified Francis Heaulme from the
photo. The interview went on:

As we drove, we talked about this and that, about me, and
Laurence. He said she was a nice piece of ass and he'd like to
give her one ... I told him it was true and that I'd like to do
things to her, I mean make love to her. I had never been to bed
with a girl. Heaulme decided we should crash into her. I agreed.
Laurence fell into the ditch ... We forced her into the car.
Heaulme shut her up with a slap. We drove for ten minutes ...
I turned into a ploughed field. She wouldn't stop yelling at me
and calling me crazy ... Heaulme was holding a flick knife ...

A flick knife ... At the end of his interview, Francis Heaulme
had taken pains to mention that he had an Opinel and not a flick
knife. Nobody had asked him anything. Changing certain details
of his crimes was typical of him.

He told me to have sex with my cousin. I didn't want to. Then
he threatened me with his knife ... Heaulme pushed me away
and took Laurence with him ... He said to me, 'If you try
anything, I'll kill her, and then I'll kill you ...' He dragged her
further away. I think Heaulme spent ten minutes alone with
Laurence ...

I stayed where I was. I heard her call for help. I didn't do anything. I began to cry ... and then he said, 'OK, it's over, don't go over there, pick up her clothes ...' We left the body where it was and drove off. I dropped him at Metz station.

'Is there anything else you want to add?'

Yes, I'd like to say that I'm not a killer, a murderer. The thing I regret that night is having met Heaulme, without knowing what he was capable of ... I'm sorry I wanted to fool around with Laurence. I didn't want to hurt her. I thought my cousin was very beautiful, I loved her and I still do. I'm prepared to prove it and to pay for the harm I did her that night. But I repeat, I don't consider myself a murderer.

I had never known Heaulme to be so much in control of events. The apparent ease with which he carried out his murderous designs was terrifying. He was a predator. From the moment he had spotted them, his two victims had little chance of getting away from him. He was brilliant at being able to sniff out others' weaknesses and understand his quarries' hidden desires and little secrets.

In this case, he knew even before meeting her what he was going to subject the girl to. For hours on end, he had fantasised about his victim, her age, her body, her personality and the way he was going to kill her. When he happened to bump into her by chance, he knew at once that he would be able to play on her cousin's repressed desire and manipulate him without danger.

Heaulme was also an opportunist killer. He rehearsed his murder fantasies for days, but it was circumstances that decided when he would carry them out. The people he met, reduced to mere objects, the places and the atmosphere were all just part of the décor, but he never forgot a single detail. They were prompts that enabled him to relive his crimes in his mind, to replay the film of those morbid scenes and feed his fantasies. But not everything was planned. When and where would he commit his murder? Circumstances provided the opportunities. He could always adapt ... Thus he left considerable room for 'improvisation'. Francis Heaulme adapted his scenarios to the behaviour of his victims, their degree of resistance or the mood of the moment.

Young Laurence Guillaume's cousin was more than a mere spectator of Heaulme's all-powerfulness. Heaulme had made the young man a full partner, the living channel through which he hoped to fulfil his sexual desires. His sexual frustration was certainly at the root of his criminal acts.

With the string of interviews, my contact with Francis Heaulme had become more and more direct. We were old acquaintances now. During one routine visit to the prisoner, this closeness nearly caused one of the worst moments of my career. It was in May 1993. That afternoon, the weather was glorious. The sun blazed in a dazzling blue sky, and spring was very much in the air. Claude, my colleague from Reims, needed to take some fresh mug shots of Francis Heaulme.

'As you're here, come with me to the prison,' he suggested. 'I've got to take Heaulme out to do some photos. It'll only take about an hour.'

I agreed and, a little later, we walked over to the prison. We were relaxed, either because of the fine weather or because of the straightforward purpose of our visit. Perhaps too relaxed. The exit formalities only took a few minutes. Soon, Claude, Francis Heaulme and I were out in the street.

'I go for walks outside!' boasted Francis Heaulme proudly, watching the prison gates close.

He was thrilled to find himself on the outside, almost free. We didn't bother to handcuff him. There were two of us, we were armed, and we were only going a hundred metres. Besides, Heaulme was on good form. He had recently told the prison psychologist that he was 'happy' there. The warders now called him by his first name, and the governor had even told him that he was 'part of the family'.

We walked on the pavement, then alongside the wall to the gendarmerie. A few dozen metres further on were our offices. The photos were taken quickly. While we were waiting, Claude offered us a drink which he brought from the investigators' lounge. Francis Heaulme gazed at us pensively, as if he were still in a daydream. Suddenly, he snapped out of his torpor and said:

'One day, between Dunkerque and Cherbourg, I strangled a tree. I squeezed, and it went all limp. It was a young one. I left it in the wild grass, by a road, twelve kilometres from the sea. That was in 1989.'

He stopped dead. As I put down my can of Coke, I said:

'Francis, can you kindly repeat that? But please, try and remember things "properly".'

'No, François, that's all I remember.'

There was no point questioning him there and then. His itinerary for 1989 had been carefully reconstructed. That year, he had not been in northern France. We would have to go backwards. With him, this had become a habit. We knew that.

Francis Heaulme presented his latest riddle, this time in a more incisive tone. He watched us with a serious expression, but did not seem perturbed. His attitude proved once again that he knew exactly what he was up to. We made no comment, thus deflating the effect of his revelation. He would not have the satisfaction of observing our reactions. Ultimately, we were copying his behaviour.

When it was time to take him back to the prison, Claude was called away by his colleagues. Another urgent case. I offered to take Heaulme back. So the pair of us set off down the empty street. On the pavement, Francis Heaulme turned to me with a smile and said, 'I could run away right now …'

'I'm sure you're not as fast as my bullets.'

I showed him the gun under my jacket.

Was he trying to be funny? But can one use the word 'humour' in connection with Francis Heaulme? The street was empty and it was as hot as summer. In the distance was a girl on a bicycle. She was wearing a light, floral print dress that billowed in the wind. A real cliché … We were outside the prison gate. I pressed the buzzer and stood in view of the little surveillance camera.

Francis Heaulme was right next to me, almost pressed up against me.

'So now you've got a cell mate. Is it hard having to share?'

He didn't reply. Without moving out of shot of the camera, I repeated my question. Still no reaction. His silence worried me. I turned towards him. His face was contorted into a grimace. That snarling grin was the embodiment of violence. He had turned pale. His sharp, penetrating gaze was riveted on the girl cycling towards us. His jaws clenched, he was breathing heavily. His hands bunched into fists. I shouted, 'Hey! Francis! Wake up! Calm down! Go easy!'

I grabbed him firmly with both hands by the collar of his jacket and flung him against the wall. He wasn't there, he was in his own world, and I had to bring him back down to earth. I shook him. He didn't budge. The girl rode past without realising anything was amiss. Without making the slightest gesture, he replied in his halting voice, 'It's OK, it's OK, don't worry.'

He carried on staring at the girl. Suddenly, he turned to me and said with a sick smile:

'François, how can you resist that?'

He stared hard at the girl again. It seemed an eternity before the gate began to open. With a sharp movement I pushed Heaulme against the corner of the gate and forced him to look me in the eyes. His face slowly relaxed. The gate finally opened. He walked through as though nothing had happened.

I stood at the entrance and watched him vanish without a word. I was furious with myself. I had not behaved appropriately. I had placed him in one of his favourite scenarios, the kind of situation which incited him to murder. The girl looked vulnerable, there was nobody in the street. I had forgotten who he was. He had sensed that I trusted him and that I'd relaxed my vigilance. His instinct had immediately come to the surface again. The vulnerability of others, that's what triggered him. Luckily, I wasn't weak enough in his eyes for him to go all the way. I swore I would never allow the situation to happen again.

I went over two phrases I had read in the most recent psychologists' reports.

Francis Heaulme shows a strong tendency to act on impulse, then having shown that he has understood the instructions, he gradually forgets them and replaces them with his own rules. The only law he follows is the law of the jungle.

He knew our rules, but preferred his world. Shouldn't he be in a psychiatric hospital rather than in prison?

On my return to the gendarmerie, I called Christophe in Rosny-sous-Bois.

'Can you do a search on the discovery of a body, in 1989, about fifteen kilometres from the sea, somewhere in France, perhaps between Dunkerque and Cherbourg? Ask Éric to contact all the stations between those two points. He can go there.'

Christophe was used to this kind of request. Especially since he had been present at an interview with Francis Heaulme. He had seen the suspect wear down the investigators and amuse himself describing his visions. He preferred to work at a distance, in the peace and quiet of his office.

'I'll call you as soon as I've got something. Oh, by the way, I'm sending you Heaulme's itinerary straight away. We've done it, I think we've reached the end, you'll see.'

And indeed, the document I received seemed very thorough. We had now located Heaulme in 400 different places where he had stayed briefly – Emmaüs communities, psychiatric hospitals, cheap hotels, camp sites, and so on. On the other hand, the number of murders that he could possibly have committed had gone down to about fifty. The pieces of the jigsaw were beginning to fit together. One by one, each piece had to be checked before we could be certain of anything.

For three years, Heaulme had been amusing himself by casually littering his interviews with the many details of his various murders. The challenge was to piece together these fragments of truth and find which murder each one related to. After months of effort, this was now done. We had an efficient tool for interpreting his words. A real key to his character. Francis Heaulme could transpose to his heart's content, we had the means to put everything back in place. Now, it didn't matter whether what he was saying was coherent or his stories plausible, the main thing was to preserve every detail of his accounts.

Unsurprisingly, I was very much in demand. In Reims, interviews with Francis Heaulme followed one after the other, charges too. I pursued my mission from city to city, from police station to gendarmerie. By the end of 1993, the list of his victims was growing longer and longer.

Lyonelle Gineste, Pont-à-Mousson, 1984

This murder was a carbon copy of that of Laurence Guillaume, only it had taken place seven years earlier. The case went back to 1984. The naked body of Lyonelle, a young hitch-hiker of seventeen, was found in a wood at Montauville, near Pont-à-Mousson. The young woman had been strangled and stabbed. Her clothes had been scattered over an area of several kilometres by the attacker or attackers. Various clues found by the investigators suggested that there were two of them.

Questioned by the investigators in charge of the case, Francis Heaulme described the events.

'I met this fellow. He called me Francis and invited me for a drink at the Bel Air café next door. When he picked up the girl hitch-hiker by the phone booth outside the baker's in Pont-à-Mousson, it annoyed me. I thought she looked like a whore. She was sexy in her black tights. She got into the back of the car, because I was next to the driver. I remember her bag, which was crescent-shaped. She shook my hand and I saw she had rings on all her fingers. I felt them too.'

A little later in the interview, he added:

'Actually, it's true he asked me to pass him the knife. It wasn't me who killed the kid. It's the other nutter. I panicked, I threw him the knife. Actually, I put it in his hand. But it wasn't me who killed her. Afterwards, it was me who got out and put the blue sweater by a tree in the forest near Atton. It's the other fellow who thought of leaving her things somewhere else … but it was I who found the place because I knew the area from riding around on my bike.'

Francis Heaulme would not give the name of his accomplice. It took the Nancy police two more months of painstaking effort to fit the pieces of the puzzle together, with my help. The 'fellow' in question was finally identified. He lived in the south of France, his name was Joseph and he was a baker. At the time of the murder, he was working with Heaulme at Lorraine TP, a civil engineering firm in Meurthe-et-Moselle. He had the same profile as young Laurence Guillaume's cousin: a slightly lost young man who was readily influenced, easy to manipulate. He too was sucked into a situation, unaware of its full horror. His interview put a different slant on things.

On 13 April 1994, Francis Heaulme and his accomplice were tried and convicted of murder.

Ghislaine Ponsard and Georgette Manesse, Charleville-Mézières, 1988

Eighty-six-year-old Ghislaine Ponsard was found stabbed to death in her kitchen. She was still wearing her raincoat. She had just come home from shopping at the market, a stone's throw from where she lived. Her trolley was full of fruit and vegetables. A few feet away, in the hall, lay Georgette Manesse, her neighbour, who acted as home help when she felt like it. She too had been stabbed. The little house in a cul-de-sac off the beaten track had been hurriedly ransacked.

Francis Heaulme was the number one suspect. A few years earlier, in Montluçon, he had been arrested after having assaulted an eighty-year-old woman who had just returned home from shopping. Fortunately, there is a gendarmes' NCO training college in

Montluçon and the streets are crawling with trainees. A group of them witnessed Francis Heaulme's attack. Caught in the act, he was sentenced to six months' imprisonment. On that occasion, his victim escaped without coming to any further harm.

After several interviews with my colleagues from Reims, Francis Heaulme was charged on 18 October 1993. The trial still hasn't taken place. And so, at the time of writing, he is presumed innocent.

Janciane Closet, Namur, January 1989

Francis Heaulme's killing spree took us to Namur, the capital of Wallonia, in Belgium, a quiet town in the Ardennes whose emblem is the snail, the symbol of tranquillity. The local police were investigating the kidnapping of a twelve-year-old girl. There was nothing to suggest that it had anything to do with Francis Heaulme, but during one interview, for no reason, he had given a very accurate description of the town. With this man, no lead could be discounted, as we had learned from past experience, especially as the Belgian inspector in charge of the kidnapping was working on another case. A murder, this time, which had shocked the people of Namur. That of a sixteen-year-old girl, who had been strangled and thrown into the river. Her body, naked to the waist, had been found on the banks of the river that flows through the region.

A Belgian delegation was expected in Reims. The inspector from Namur only had an international letter rogatory. Consequently, the case of the murdered teenager could not be mentioned.

The interview took place at the regional police criminal investigation headquarters. Accompanied by Ange-Marie, I introduced the Belgian investigators to Francis Heaulme. He liked their Belgian accent. He voluntarily replied to the customary questions, with almost too much alacrity. I had the sense that my presence encouraged him. He commented:

'Why don't you ask François what I've done, he knows everything. He says the name of the town, and then I remember.'

'That's true, Francis, you tend to remember things more easily when I'm there. I wonder why that is.'

He knew exactly what I meant. My presence restricted his scope for manipulation. He could not change his mind about the cases I knew about. Very calmly, he continued his account. He described the city and confirmed that he had been there with a friend 'who picked up a girl in a square'.

The Belgian investigators did not have enough information to support or contradict his explanations, as Francis Heaulme had long since realised.

They mentioned the district where the girl had vanished, but that did not interest him. The interview went on interminably and soon became bogged down. I tried to help the Belgian police officers. I asked Heaulme what had made him talk to us about Namur before, but to no avail. He was making fun of us. It was best to halt the interview.

Suddenly, Francis Heaulme changed the subject. He started talking about one of his friends, called Raymond, to whom he had given his Opinel knife. The next day, he claimed, his friend used it to kill a girl in Blainville-sur-l'Eau. He had been arrested. Was this another coded message? Francis Heaulme was showing off. What was behind this provocation? He clearly had nothing to do with the kidnapping of the teenage girl. The Belgian inspectors decided to call it a day. Before leaving, they asked him one last thing.

'We're going to ask you a terrible question, which is: how would you kill a little girl?'

Francis Heaulme turned to me in amusement. What's so 'terrible' about that, he seemed to want to say. After a long silence, he announced:

'In Namur? I would strangle her like a maniac, then I'd throw the body into the river.'

Francis Heaulme's answer left us stunned. He clearly wanted to talk about something else. We were convinced that he was referring to the case of the girl in the river. Without a letter rogatory, my colleagues had to stop there. They left, certain they knew the identity of the killer they were seeking, but absolutely unable to prove it. Heaulme would never refer to that affair again.

Despite the suspicions hanging over him, he was never charged.

After carrying out various checks, one detail continued to bother me, and still does today. This Raymond to whom Heaulme had given his knife does actually exist. He was even convicted in 1990 for the murder of a young girl, in Blainville-sur-l'Eau, as Francis had told us. Give or take a few details, the Moulin Blanc killer had been there, on the eve of the murder, his name in black and white in the register of the town's Emmaüs community.

Joris Viville, Port-Grimaud, April 1989

The 'young one' left in the wild grass by Francis Heaulme was called Joris Viville. A nine-year-old boy of Flemish origin, kidnapped from a camp site at Port-Grimaud in April 1989. After Brest, this was the fourth charge for a murder committed between April and August 1989.

Joris was kidnapped at around 5.30 p.m. on 5 April 1989. His clothes were soon discovered under a bridge on the road to Fréjus. His naked body was found seventeen days later. The child was lying on a bed of ferns, slightly set back from the road, behind a forest-fire-prevention water tank, well sheltered from view.

He had not been killed on the spot, but just deposited there. It was an out-of-the-way place, even more remote than the sites of previous murders. He had been strangled, but his body had strange puncture marks that the autopsy was unable to identify.

Apart from the mode of operation, the crime did not initially seem to bear Heaulme's stamp. First of all, little Joris's clothes found under the bridge could only have been thrown from a car. And secondly, on the day of the kidnapping, Heaulme had an alibi – he had been staying as an in-patient at the psychiatric hospital of La Fontonne, in Antibes, eighty kilometres away from the camp site. The only connection was that the hospital had booked some caravans there to give some of the patients a holiday.

Furthermore, in the hospital records, a nurse had mentioned something of great interest, dated the day the boy vanished. The report concerns the arrival during the evening of Francis Heaulme. It reads: 'Patient arrived alone, state of anxiety: "+ + +". He refuses to go and watch TV and says he killed someone in Port-Antibes.'

Unfortunately, the hospital staff did not attempt to probe further. The next day, everybody read the papers, but as nobody had been found dead in the port of Antibes, the business was forgotten. Worse, he was given a train ticket back to Metz.

It is hard to understand why nobody from the hospital came forward when the boy's body was found a couple of weeks later. Interviews were arranged, hospital personnel were questioned, but they all took shelter behind patient confidentiality. There was nothing the investigating magistrate in charge of the case could do.

It seemed very likely that Heaulme had an accomplice.

He gave the investigators from Aix-en-Provence his version of events.

'I remember the tree went all limp. I strangled something that became someone, but I don't remember where. I don't remember. I only know that it was in 1989. I don't remember, but let me explain. I had a fit, I hugged a tree, and I saw a shadow, somebody standing in front of me, I saw red, but I don't know who I killed. The person was in front of me, I don't know if it was a man or a woman, I know I could see the sea, there was a little road with trees, I don't remember where it was ... I was in the south, somewhere between Marseille and Nice ... when I came to, I was squeezing a tree between my hands. I had a fit, it was silent and the tree fell. When the tree fell, it became a person. I didn't touch it. I left.'

Later during questioning, he explained, 'I went off with another patient from the hospital. I know he had a goatee ... We went to the shop to buy some beer ... Then we went to drink it, further away. Someone was throwing stones at us. My companion went over to him and they got into a fight. I stepped in and squeezed his throat. He collapsed ...'

And then, after that:

'Now I'm going to tell you the truth. I went out with a male nurse ... We sat on the rocks. I drank a beer and we chatted. Suddenly, we saw a youth coming towards us. I don't know where he appeared from, but he started throwing stones at us and shouting abuse. He had an accent. I couldn't understand what he was saying.'

The victim was a young Belgian who spoke only Flemish.

'I know the other fellow hit the kid with something he was holding, he hit him all over, on the head and all over his body. I tried to step in, and that's when I squeezed a tree ... He undressed the kid ... I said to him, "Don't undress the kid, people will think it's a rape." I don't touch kids. I don't like homosexuals. I'm not interested in sex. The only thing that matters is work, besides, I'm impotent ... Afterwards, he threw the kid's clothes some ten metres from the car ...'

Legally, this statement contained no concrete proof. Francis Heaulme was now so accustomed to being questioned that he had become adept at interrogation techniques. He could see through the investigators' questions like a hardened criminal. However, I advised my colleagues from Aix-en-Provence to continue. I believed they were close to success.

Unfortunately, the subsequent interviews ended in confusion. Several times, Francis Heaulme gave the names of accomplices, which he hastily changed. The first concrete elements he supplied were three sketches. One pinpointed the camp site where the boy had been kidnapped, the others the scene of the crime and the place where the body had been found. Yet this was still insufficient. The names Heaulme gave confused the investigators more than anything else. My strategy of writing everything down had its limitations.

Then another factor disrupted everything. The press publicised the suspicions surrounding Heaulme. In prison, he was often threatened. Child murderers are despised by the other prisoners. Very quickly he clammed up and refused to talk. His Parisian counsel, Maître Pierre Gonzalez de Gaspard, was now beginning to talk of unprecedented police intimidation. He believed that his client was 'confessing because he was unable to withstand the pressure of detention'. Some of the cases, based on scant evidence, were lacking in detail, which did not help matters.

From then on, Heaulme systematically retracted his statements. His counsel was in full agreement with him. When he killed alone, we soon drew a blank. The successive charges had only one effect: media exposure. Francis Heaulme enjoyed the status of serial offender. His avowed and putative crimes made him a media figure. More than ever, he was mocking us.

The situation rapidly went downhill. In less than two weeks, the mood deteriorated. People began to doubt. Colonel F of the Rennes unit was replaced. His successor was by no means a stranger to me. He was the former commander of the Brest company, the man who, in 1989, had refused to believe that Francis Heaulme might be implicated in the Moulin Blanc murder ... The minute his feet were under the desk, he formally summoned me to inform me that he would do everything in his power to have me removed from his department. He disliked the way I worked. A promising start ...

At the same time, in Paris, the officer who had set up the Heaulme unit was also replaced. In the face of mounting media pressure, his boss, a colonel, also summoned me. I presented myself at headquarters, accompanied by a colleague. We were shown up to the VIP floor. We walked along a spotless red carpet. I didn't know what to think. The man who received us was the head of the gendarmerie's criminal investigation bureau, he was an important figure. His greeting was artificially cordial.

'Come in, do sit down. I've heard so much about you.'

Not mentioning the purpose of the meeting was not necessarily a good sign. I sat down. The colonel went on, 'Would you like a coffee?'

Immediately, a captain appeared from nowhere with four cups of coffee. Amazing. What did he want?

'I'd like you to know, Chief Abgrall, that all of us here are very satisfied with your work. Oh, yes, absolutely. However, we have to be clear about how far we can go. You've seen the press: Heaulme is retracting his statements. Is he really the author of these murders? What will happen when he appears in court? If he ends up being acquitted, it will make the gendarmerie look bad, do you see?'

I replied:

'There is absolutely no doubt about the Moulin Blanc case, there's nothing to fear. Heaulme is well and truly implicated in the cases he's been charged with, it's up to the defence to prove the contrary.'

'Perhaps, but you never know. The gendarmerie is going to close down the special unit. Besides, officially, we never seconded you. Our conversation didn't happen. If you are charged, consider hiring a defence counsel.'

He was reneging on everything, with no concessions. For me, it was unthinkable. I looked at my colleague and we left. As we reached the exit, I said:

'Tell me, did you hear what I heard? Mission impossible. It's over!'

A few days later, in Rennes, my new boss ordered me to continue assisting the Aix-en-Provence unit, even if it meant being involved in the interview.

'I can't, there's no unit any more. What's more, there never was one, apparently. By the way, Francis Heaulme has been transferred to Aix and I don't have the authority to interview him.'

I knew that in Aix, the team was experiencing major difficulties with the case, but I wanted to show my displeasure. Briefing investigators is very different from interviewing. Everybody has their own approach, and this time there was a lot at stake, given the lack of support. If he gave me detailed confessions without his accomplice being identified, I would come in for heavy criticism. I didn't want to be the fall guy, either.

I stood my ground for a few days, until headquarters gave me a temporary secondment to the Aix-en-Provence unit. There was now no legal obstacle to my interviewing Francis Heaulme in person. The investigating magistrate of the Draguignan high court was unaware of these manoeuvres. She approved the initiative and requested my direct help with the case.

On 13 December 1993 at 2.30 p.m., in the offices of the Draguignan brigade, my Aix counterpart, Francis Heaulme and I brought this case to a swift close.

In less than two hours, Joris's murderer gave us all the details of his crime. The object he used as a weapon was a small screwdriver. We did not know that. On the other hand, he refused once again to name his accomplice. He was adamant. Even so, we had a very good lead. We knew the identity of the accomplice but we had no proof. We had to keep looking.

The same day, Francis Heaulme was charged. The case was officially closed.

To my great surprise, the unit was kept going for another six months to give the last teams the opportunity to question the killer. Among them was the Lille criminal investigation unit, which had been waiting its turn for several months. This time the victim was a man, Jean Rémy, whose body had been found in early 1992 on a beach in Boulogne-sur-Mer. This murder had been committed the weekend before Heaulme had been arrested in Alsace.

To my astonishment, I heard him tell the investigators:

'François told me he was going to come back and arrest me. So I went to see the sea, at Boulogne-sur-Mer ... and I killed a man. It was an accident, he wanted to die.'

' I went to see the sea ...' A phrase he'd come out with nearly two years earlier, on the day he had been arrested. The announcement of a murder, committed while he was waiting for me. I remembered that moment with the utmost clarity, his fixed stare, my bafflement. Retrospectively, it sent a chill down my spine.

The incident has since been reconstructed. Jean Rémy, sixty-five years old, retired, was grieving after the premature death of his wife, which he had never got over. He had decided to set off on a journey retracing their past, in a final tribute to her. He wanted to go back to Le Touquet, where he and his wife had spent their most wonderful holiday. An inhabitant of the Somme region, he took the evening train from Amiens. This was Friday 4 January 1992. Unfortunately, Jean Rémy fell asleep and woke up at the end of the line, Boulogne-sur-Mer. There was no way back until the following morning. Dispirited, he was wandering along the strand, at a loss, when he met Francis Heaulme, who had come to see the sea ... Very quickly, the man whom I was to arrest three days later noticed Jean Rémy's disarray. They talked, the widower unburdened himself, described his wife and how hard it was for him to carry on without her. They walked together for quite a while, as far as the beach. When they reached the end, well out of sight, Heaulme killed him.

That May 1994, Francis Heaulme had already been charged with eight murders. The list of similar crimes still included a number of murders that corresponded to the killer's fantasies. So, despite the announced closure of the unit, I travelled around France one last time and gave Francis Heaulme's itinerary to the units concerned. I tried once again to explain the weirdness of his behaviour and the complexity of his personality. Some listened to me, others didn't. There was no time left for me to convince them. Now I know that most of these murders have been forgotten.

PART THREE

An unfinished story

11

First trial

The beginning of January 1994 was a whirl of press conferences given by Maître Pierre Gonzalez de Gaspard. Francis Heaulme's counsel was continually trumpeting to the media that his client had not killed Aline Pérès. Nor had he committed any other murders. These repeated declarations eventually bore fruit. On the eve of the first trial, which took place in Quimper, Heaulme was described in most of the newspaper articles as a simple 'confused vagrant'. The same words kept recurring. They pointed at me. It was not rare to read that 'Abgrall made me talk, he pressurised me until I couldn't take any more,' or: 'I had faith and then I found myself caught up in the system.'

Considering how little backing I enjoyed, I stayed on my guard in face of this turn of events, even though I realised that this was part of his defence strategy. This was not the most worrying thing. On the dawn of the opening day of the trial, 'The

Gaul', the key man, the only witness to the murder of Aline, had once again gone missing. Francis Heaulme's lawyer knew it, and was now intimating that his client, who denied his involvement in the murder, had an alibi. In the eyes of the law, the disappearance of 'The Gaul' was tantamount to flight, an offence punishable by a prison sentence. Under these conditions, I felt pretty nervous at the prospect of taking the witness stand opposite Pierre Gonzalez de Gaspard, especially as I was not allowed to allude to the other cases in order to elaborate on the killer's personality. Only the Moulin Blanc investigation could be referred to in the trial.

28 January 1994, 9 a.m. The lobby of the modest Law Courts in Quimper was packed. Potential jurors, witnesses, experts, the victim's relatives and those of Francis Heaulme mingled in silence with the usual onlookers. Already the media pack, brandishing cameras and mikes, were trying to get exclusives.

Everyone was waiting for the heavy court room doors to open, but they remained resolutely shut. A new passage had been specially created to channel the flow of people in and out of the building. Everyone had to go through the metal detector. These unusual measures and the huge media interest increased my apprehension. I wasn't thrilled at having to cross the lobby in uniform. I needed calm, the stakes were too high. I slipped discreetly into the courts through a side door that was reserved for detainees. Together with Éric from the Brest criminal investigation unit, who had also been summonsed to testify, I stayed out in a corridor until the waiting room emptied.

Francis Heaulme arrived, escorted by four police officers. He entered quickly, and passed close to where we stood, his hands bound, led on a chain held firmly by a police officer. As he passed me, he shouted:

'Oh, hello François! It wasn't me. I didn't do Brest!'

I watched him disappear into the little room reserved for the defendant, telling myself that this trial was going to be extremely difficult. I began to feel the pressure. When the time came, we entered the court room unobtrusively. It was full to bursting point. High up on the ceiling, neon lights glared. On a side wall, small windows looked out onto a corridor. Faces were pressed behind every pane. The wooden benches had places reserved for relatives, the press and a privileged few. Everyone else remained standing, crammed behind the guard-rail on the back row of benches. There was a heavy police presence. Curious members of the public had to remain outside for lack of space. The opening of the trial resembled a theatre performance.

A bell rang. The usher announced the arrival of the judge. The court rose. Two female magistrates flanked the presiding judge, who wore a red robe. The counsel for the prosecution followed, at a slight distance. Everyone sat down again, and there was silence. The presiding judge spoke into the microphone:

'Bring in the defendant!'

Francis Heaulme, handcuffed and heavily guarded, had to walk the width of the court room to reach the dock, where his handcuffs were removed. The flashbulbs started popping and the cameras whirring. The presiding judge soon put a stop to the photography, and some of the press were already leaving.

The usher began the roll-call of jurors, then, immediately, the random selection process began. Statistics have shown that certain make-ups of jury tend to be more sympathetic either towards the defence or the prosecution depending on the age, sex and profession of the jurors. The drawing of jurors' names began and the counsel for the prosecution and Pierre Gonzalez de Gaspard then opened the subtle game of challenging. The people called by the usher crossed the court room one by one, watched by all present. Without knowing why, some were challenged off. The jury ended up being composed of six women and three men. Then the witnesses were called. When 'The Gaul's' name was read out, there was no reply. The presiding judge ordered an immediate search to be launched. When I signalled my presence, the whole court turned around in unison. There was a brief murmur. I couldn't fathom the meaning.

The roll-call continued. Only eight witnesses would appear: the three experts – psychiatrists and psychologists – to testify with regard to the defendant's personality, the forensic scientist to state the causes of death, 'The Gaul', Éric and myself for the prosecution, and Christine, the defendant's sister, as a character witness. This was very few for a court of assizes. The other testimonies gathered during the investigation were to be read out by the presiding judge during the course of the trial. Then, with great solemnity, Maître Gonzalez de Gaspard spoke:

'Your Honour, Francis Heaulme deserves more than two

days' trial. He is appearing here solely for the Brest case, yet everyone sees him as a serial killer. The jury has been influenced, as the presence of the media illustrates. I demand due calm. For this reason, I request that the trial be postponed.'

The counsel then handed his written conclusions to the judge. A murmur rippled through the court. The first speech, the first interruption. Pierre Gonzalez de Gaspard had got off to a successful start. After a few minutes' deliberation, the judge decided to uphold the trial. He informed the witnesses of the order in which they would be called. Éric and I were asked to appear the following day at 2 p.m. We left the court – witnesses are not allowed to attend the trial, even if it is public – and hurried back to the Quimper gendarmerie, where several of our colleagues were following the proceedings on the radio. They told us that Heaulme's counsel was claiming that his client had admitted to the crime under police pressure. They made noises of encouragement but deep down they were relieved not to be in our shoes. With a half-smile, one of them brought me a message from my new departmental boss: 'Commanding officer and criminal investigation unit commander will attend trial Quimper court of assizes, reserve front row seats.' Like at the theatre ... That was all I needed. Let them make their own arrangements!

Meanwhile, the confrontation between Francis Heaulme and the experts had begun. Some of my colleagues attended the trial, and after the verdict was announced, they faithfully relayed the exchanges back to me. The psychiatrist had been the first to speak. He declared:

'Despite his slightly half-witted air, Francis Heaulme is of normal intelligence ... He is not subnormal as defined by Article 64 of the penal code ... Alcohol makes him feel all-powerful. He identifies with his terrifying, violent father.'

The interpretation of the Rorschach test inkblots was referred to and the expert emphasised the fascination with which Francis Heaulme described them: 'It flows, it's red, you can smell it, it's alive.' And lastly, with a hint of irony, he spoke of the defendant's 'unfortunate' destiny – in the words of Francis Heaulme, 'Wherever I go, a murder takes place.'

The other two doctors described his profound discomfort regarding his sexuality. One of them declared:

'Everything concerning the body increases his sense of insecurity and provokes an aggressive defence at the same time as arousing desire.'

'What can you tell us about the defendant's "vision" of the murder?' the judge asked the experts.

'It is more like a defence strategy,' they replied.

The experts concluded that Heaulme was conscious of his actions; he was not insane, but he was dangerous and, given his personality, he could indeed have been the author of the murder. The judge then turned to the defendant and invited him to speak. After a brief silence, Francis Heaulme spoke to the psychiatrist.

'I have two questions: Am I mad? Am I dangerous?'

Slightly at a loss, the doctor indicated that he had just answered those questions. Pierre Gonzalez de Gaspard seized the chance to jump in again:

'It is perfectly clear that my client is mentally deficient. It is easy to see that there's something wrong with Francis Heaulme. Everything suggests that this man does not grasp the reality of the world around him.'

In vain. This time, the Moulin Blanc killer's counsel was unable to undermine the psychologists' testimonies. In the court room, nobody seemed inclined to believe that the presumed murderer was not responsible for his actions.

The afternoon session was devoted to examining the defendant's personality. For several hours, the judge fired endless questions at Francis Heaulme, who replied. By the end, the contrast with the morning's proceedings was striking. The media all reported his declarations in the witness box. The man knew how to pull the wool over people's eyes. A number of journalists were beginning to ask questions.

Francis Heaulme talks about his inner turmoil in a soft voice. He is precise and deferential. He told his life story – the beatings, bereavement, the aimless wandering and the alcohol, but then denied murdering Aline Pérès. A puzzle.

Or:

Heaulme is a man who is to be pitied rather than feared. Labelled 'the French serial killer', Francis Heaulme could just be a blip in the criminal annals of the late twentieth century.

As the day drew to a close, it seemed to me that the absence of 'The Gaul' was increasingly ominous, as Francis Heaulme and his counsel were turning things on their head. In my hotel room, I reread the records of the Moulin Blanc investigation in detail. I learned nothing new, but it kept me busy.

The next morning, I returned to wait at the Quimper gendarmerie. The colleagues who had attended the trial informed me that my superiors had sat on the bench near the victim's family.

The morning was devoted to questioning Christine, the defendant's sister. She spoke of the poverty of their family life, the death of their mother and the problems they had faced as a result. Christine Heaulme was moving, for their life truly had been hard. She had not been able to hold back her tears, nor had some of the jury. This was the moment chosen by the defence counsel to speak. The minute her testimony was over, Francis Heaulme again stated his innocence. The judge began questioning him about the murder, emphasising, for example, the accuracy of the sketch.

'It was imaginary,' replied Heaulme, 'it's a coincidence if my sketch is the same as the scene of the crime … I was in hospital in Quimper on Sunday 14 May 1989, and I didn't leave the building. I was not involved in this crime. I talked about a vision I'd had on Saturday 13 May on the beach where the murder took place. I had taken Tranxene 50 with a litre of beer, and, while I was asleep, I saw a fair-haired man stabbing a woman with a knife … I read about the murder in the newspaper … when I talked, it was to please officer Abgrall. He hypnotises me!'

The counsel emphasised his client's psychological frailty:

'He couldn't cope with the pressure of being in custody, he's a liar, a fantasist ...'

He went on, stressing that the investigators had suggested details of the case to Francis Heaulme, perhaps even unconsciously, through the questions they asked him. The atmosphere was becoming more heated. It was 12.30 when my colleagues from Quimper returned. They immediately told us about the mood in the court room.

'Heaulme's counsel is attacking you, he speaks of that "devil Abgrall",' said one of them. 'What's more, he went for you so savagely, that your bosses left and went back to Rennes.'

It goes without saying that I had no appetite for lunch. I was growing impatient to have my say, the waiting was becoming unbearable.

At 1.45 p.m., when we arrived at the court, a crowd even bigger than yesterday's was waiting in the lobby. Even more daunting, the court room was already full to bursting point. We went directly into the witnesses' waiting room. This was it. A police officer on sentry duty saw to it that we stayed put and did not communicate with the outside.

The area was small, but roomy enough for Éric and me. We did not know how the trial was progressing. We waited, and the minutes dragged by. We did not speak. We didn't admit it, but we were tense. From time to time, the police officer left us to go and watch the trial for a few minutes. He kept coming and going, and each time he opened the door I expected the usher to call me to the witness stand. Two hours passed thus. Then the police officer returned and asked:

'Which one's Abgrall?'

Taken by surprise, I replied:

'I am.'

'Whew,' he said, shaking his right hand, 'things are hotting up in there!'

Then he hurried off again. I looked at Éric, dumbfounded. Then the hearing was suspended. Ten minutes went by and the door swung open to reveal 'The Gaul', in a blue anorak. I was totally taken by surprise, but felt a surge of relief. The police officer went back to his post, we were forbidden to talk to each other. 'The Gaul' turned to him and tried, anxiously, to explain his absence.

'I was at the Emmaüs community of Château-Gontier when a mate who was watching TV turned round and told me I was wanted by the police. We called the gendarmerie, and here I am. But I haven't done anything, honest!'

Less than five minutes later, the usher led him into the court room. The press described what happened next. On catching sight of him, Francis Heaulme did not bat an eyelid, whereas 'The Gaul' was visibly ill at ease.

'Do you know the defendant?' asked the judge.

'Yes,' replied 'The Gaul'.

'What about the victim?'

'I knew her too.'

Then came a trying examination. The witness had difficulty

understanding the questions. He seemed frightened and mumbled his answers.

'I met Heaulme at the beach. I was on the rocks. He saw that girl. He went over to her, and that's when I left to get a train.'

As the questions became more precise, the witness became more specific.

'I'd been on the beach for several days, and I'd noticed Aline, who sunbathed by the rocks. I met Heaulme in the nearby Emmaüs community. That Sunday, Heaulme had come up to me. He was drunk. I told him there was no point hassling the girl. He went up to her and grabbed her by the throat. I saw him do that when I looked over my shoulder. Heaulme was all wound up, you could see it in his eyes. I left. I was afraid he'd do the same to me.'

The judge reminded the court that Francis Heaulme had told the gendarmes that the witness had been present for the entire time, but 'The Gaul' stated that he had left at that point. Maître Gonzalez de Gaspard spoke and referred to failure to assist a person in danger.★ The witness replied that his conscience was clear, even though it was true that he had not taken the precaution of calling the police. Heaulme rose and spoke too:

'I don't know this man. I've never seen him before.'

The prosecution took the floor:

'Then why did you go over and shake his hand on the day the reconstruction was staged?'

★ Translator's note: Under the French penal code, '*non-assistance à personne en danger*' is counted an offence.

211

Heaulme replied:

'To please François Abgrall.'

The witness was then free to retire. This time, the usher called my name. In the corridor I passed 'The Gaul' and the police officer escorting him. He gave me a smile, proffered his hand and said: 'Go on, my friend!' In passing, he slipped into my hand a tiny Emmaüs community calendar. I didn't have time just then to dwell on this gesture or its signification. I later realised that actually he was trying to give me the only wealth he had, his calling card, the symbol of his respectability.

I entered the court room. The witnesses' entrance faced the dock. Francis Heaulme was in front of me, our eyes met and he did not reply to my discreet 'Hello'. There was absolute silence, the only sound my footsteps on the parquet floor. I felt as though time had stopped.

The judge asked me to give my evidence. I began, and slowly described the investigation, the leads we'd followed up and the reasons for ruling them out. Then the similarity between the alibis for this murder and for the one in Courthézon, near Avignon, which confirmed my suspicions. And lastly, I described at length the behaviour of Francis Heaulme during his interviews. I reproduced the chilling gesture showing the neck hold on the victim as he had demonstrated it in Strasbourg. I reminded the court that the forensic scientist had drawn our attention to it at the time. The judge requested clarification. Then I mentioned the sketch and the spontaneity of the confessions.

A few moments later, it was defence counsel Pierre Gonzalez de Gaspard's turn to question me:

'Were you, Mr Abgrall, and this is very important, on first-name terms with my client during these interviews?'

I replied in the affirmative to the judge, as is customary. The lawyer was jubilant and went on, addressing the jury:

'You heard, this gendarme was on first-name terms with Francis Heaulme throughout the interviews. Heaulme, who can't cope with pressure, as the psychiatrists have explained, this fabricator who accuses himself of crimes that he did not commit, this gullible person. What credibility can his confessions have?'

Amazed at the violence of his outburst, I couldn't help replying:

'It was Francis Heaulme who started calling me by my first name. Ask him.'

Without even being invited, Francis Heaulme spoke and confirmed this was so, but his counsel insisted:

'Mr Abgrall, you are a likeable man. Your whole attitude shows it. I am convinced that my client's confessions were obtained through trust and kindness. Could that not be called psychological abuse?'

'You know, if all I had to do was use his first name and be nice to him to get him to talk to me about all the murders he's been involved in, then it wouldn't have taken me three years and we wouldn't be where we are today.'

In the end, we left it at that.

Once I had given my evidence, I decided to stay and listen to the hearing. The testimony of Éric, the last witness, was quick and confirmed the defendant's behaviour. Even so, I was worried. I could sense that the defence counsel's repeated attacks had unsettled the jury. Nothing was certain.

Then came the closing speeches. Francis Heaulme's lawyer tried to minimise the impact of 'The Gaul's' testimony and cleverly to sow doubt in the jury's minds by reversing the roles. According to him, Heaulme could not have killed, as he had been in hospital. If he described the Moulin Blanc murder in such detail, it was because someone had told him about it. Probably the killer himself. Heaulme not having been present, there was only one person who admitted having been near the victim at the time of the crime: 'The Gaul'. This carefully orchestrated demonstration had the desired effect. In the court room, doubt could be read on many faces. For a few moments, I envisaged the worst: Francis Heaulme's acquittal.

The judge and jury retired. An hour and a half later, the court filled up once more. Verdict: twenty years' imprisonment. It was not the maximum sentence, but justice had been done. The convict showed no emotion. His gaze blank, he gave nothing away, as if he had withdrawn deep into himself, probably into that universe filled with morbid dreams where he was no longer that unloved creature forsaken by the real world.

In any case, Aline Pérès's killer was not about to claim any more victims, especially as further trials were in the offing. Probably further convictions too. I was relieved. Francis Heaulme's killing spree had come to a full stop here, in Quimper. At least, that is what I believed.

12

The last visit

8 June 1994 is a date that will always stand out in my mind.
After tracking Aline Pérès's killer for months, then interviewing
him, questioning him and trying to decipher him for five long
years, I was now being asked to bring my investigation to an
end. This was therefore the last afternoon that I would spend
with Francis Heaulme. A last visit, a mixture of disappointment
and relief. Disappointment because I was now forced to abandon
my investigations into the crimes of this man, relief too because
those years spent on the killer's trail had sometimes been a
burden.

As usual, we met in the tiny visiting room of Reims prison
which could barely accommodate the two of us. The rapid
handshake I insisted on always had the same effect on Heaulme.
Some psychotics experience physical contact as an attack on
their person. And yet it was a sort of game between us. Visibly

preoccupied, the minute he entered the room the words spilled out:

'On Wednesday, I was going up the stairs, minding my own business, and an Arab – he'd been transferred – smashed a chair over my head. I wasn't hurt at all. Then he started kicking me in the spine. It was black and blue for a while. The warders came rushing over to separate us at once. I was wearing my watch and the strap's bust.'

'Why did he do that?'

'Because of little Joris …'

So that was his problem. I had not come to listen to him moan about his personal difficulties, but to tell him I would not be seeing him ever again. I knew very well that our paths would cross again at future trials, but we would not have the same opportunity for these cosy little conversations.

'Listen, my investigation is over, it's going to be very difficult for me to come and see you.'

'Is it the holidays now?'

'No, that's not it, I won't be able to come and see you any more.'

He wasn't listening to me but started talking about his sister's last visit. She was going to take part in a TV programme. He was no different, his mind was always elsewhere. This was perhaps the moment to pick up the thread.

'Francis, have you told your sister everything you've done?'

After a silence, he said:

'I've half told her …'

'Why don't you tell her?'

'No!'

'She'll find out.'

'She already knows, she already knows, from the papers, she already knows!'

'I don't know what you want, Francis, but you're bound to have more difficult trials, and you're likely to receive much longer sentences because you're lying. Of course it's up to you, but if I were you, I'd say, "Yes, I did that to such-and-such a person."'

'What is Article 122?' he burst out.

Article 122 rather than any other ... It was no coincidence. This article of the penal code covers diminished criminal responsibility. Its application may enable the author of a crime to be sent to an appropriate psychiatric establishment rather than to prison. I knew what he was getting at. He was lucid. The psychiatrists deemed him responsible for his actions in the eyes of the law. That meant he would be locked up. So I preferred not to answer his question.

I allowed silence to reign. It went on for ages, and then Francis Heaulme spoke again. He referred to the Pont-à-Mousson murder, that of Lyonelle Gineste found dead in the middle of a field in 1984. I was no longer interested. He had already gone into the details with the Nancy investigators. I wanted to tell him that now everyone was familiar with his little games he might do better to change his attitude and stop this futile game of cat and mouse.

The Pont-à-Mousson case, presented as the first time he had acted out his murder fantasies, had the indisputable hallmark of a practised killer, as several of us had noted. This was not Heaulme's first crime. Soon, other investigators would come and interview him. I tried to get him to understand this.

'I'm telling you straight, Francis, there are lots of other cases that have come to light, for which you haven't been questioned, as you know only too well.'

'Well, you're questioning me, aren't you?'

'Yes, and you're going to start playing your games again. Why don't you tell me everything?'

'I don't know … I haven't got the guts.'

Before even asking the questions, I could envisage the answers. Francis Heaulme would never open up, it was clear. But I was glad to talk to him without there being anything at stake, without the pressure. We continued our conversation, which invariably returned to the murders. He never let up. He explained to me in detail things that he had not said when in custody and withdrew statements he had made about other cases where he had given ample proof of his involvement to the investigators. He was still trying to convince, probably himself as much as anyone else. I wondered whether he realised how inconsistent he was. In any case, he knew exactly when he could adopt this type of behaviour: when he was outside the frame. Outside the frame of custody, at a time when he could say anything without there being any risk. It had become a reflex with him. He continued his monologue.

'I know I won't go to prison. I'll be sent to a psychiatric hospital … That's what I need.'

I remained silent, but I believed he was right. And yet it was too late. The experts had decided otherwise. Psychiatry could do nothing for him, one of them had declared in the witness box in the Finistère court of assizes. Before returning to Rennes and washing my hands of him once and for all, I wanted to discuss the real motivation for his crimes. In spite of everything I knew about this character, the secret still escaped me.

'Do you know why you commit these crimes, do you have an idea?'

'It's because of the alcohol, and my visions. But since I've been taking this new treatment, I've been better.'

'And do you remember all the murders?'

'It's buried in my mind.'

'Do you relive them sometimes?'

'Yeah.'

'And what do you feel?'

'Nothing, nothing.'

'And were all the murders quick?'

'Yeah ... I don't remember.'

'And did the people always try to run away?'

'Yeah!'

'Were there any that you missed?'

'Missed? Sometimes, yeah, several.'

'Which ones did you miss?'

'Just people ... nobody special.'

'When did you begin to have problems?'

'When we ... In 1984 ... I was in the car.'

He was harking back to the killing of Lyonelle Gineste again. Once again, he thought it would be useful to remind me that he was only the witness to the girl's murder.

'Did you have any problems before 1984?'

'Before? No, I was working.'

I didn't believe him and told him so. I advised him to talk to his lawyer about it. To tell him everything, even if some things had to be kept secret, so that at least somebody would be aware of the problem. Francis Heaulme remained unreceptive. Even after five years, it seemed impossible to break through his defences. He returned to the Quimper court sentence, wanted the verdict quashed. He still thought he had a chance of being sent to a psychiatric hospital. I continued:

'I have to go back to Brittany. I'm going home for a while. You've led me a dance, you've travelled all over, haven't you?'

'That's all finished. It was the alcohol,' he added fatalistically. 'Like I told the psychiatrists, it's the alcohol that does the bad things,' he said speaking of the murders.

'Have you ever told a single person about everything that you've done?'

'No. I keep it all to myself.'

'What about your friend Raymond?'

The Raymond in question had been convicted of the murder of a girl walking home from a party in Blainville-sur-l'Eau in 1990. Raymond was staying at the local Emmaüs community which Francis Heaulme had left the day before the murder. The day before, as in Brest. The killer repeated his friend's parting words:

'Raymond said to me, "If you leave, I'll do something stupid!" and he did. It was nothing to do with me.'

Then, for no reason, Francis Heaulme changed the subject.

He told me, utterly convinced, how he had had a conversation with the father of young Laurence Guillaume, killed in Metz.

'It was during the reconstruction. I went up to him and told him everything. How his daughter had died, by accident.'

I knew he was lying to me, that everything he said was untrue. He had never spoken to this man, but I let him go on. I was still observing him. Actually he was giving the version he had served up to the investigators a few weeks earlier. He could not help presenting himself as the person thanks to whom the truth could be established, the good guy, and not the author of all those horrific crimes. His way of deflecting the conversation was a sign that things were getting too close for comfort. As I said nothing, he carried on. Now, he was giving me very precise explanations of what had happened in the gym in Périgueux, where the young conscript had been murdered. He described more vividly than ever how the victim had died. In his perversity, he knew that there was no danger. I let him speak without interrupting him, and then I asked:

'With these "cock-ups" of yours, have there been more women or more men?'

'Men!'

After a silence, I asked:

'There are more men?'

'Yeah.'

'But so far you've only mentioned one. What happened to the others?'

Francis Heaulme realised what he had just told me. He stared at me coldly and replied:

'I don't remember.'

He immediately went back to the assault he'd suffered in prison. That was how he regained his composure. Once again, he had deftly deflected the conversation. He started talking about a woman who was moved by his fate and had written to him. I jumped at the opportunity:

'What does she write to you about?'

'Well, she says I must tell the truth, that I must tell the truth.'

'The truth, Francis. I know you, you'll never tell the truth. It's not in your nature, am I right?'

He sat staring at me without replying. I told him that was not the reason I was there. I reminded him that during our last conversation he had asked me to come back, so I was coming back before returning to Brittany once and for all. With the utmost seriousness, he then asked me to investigate some of the mail he had received. He had the feeling that some of the letters came from journalists looking for information ... That made me smile, briefly. Then we talked about his family life, the death of his mother when he was twenty-six years old.

He spoke about his father, whom he resented for having made a new life. He claimed he had written to him, but had never received a reply. Then he talked about his chronic alcoholism again, which he said started when he was seventeen or eighteen. Inevitably, even though we avoided the word, we came back to his crimes:

'When you did those things, did you forget about them straight away?'

'Yeah.'

'What happened?'

'Well … I'd see red. Pow! … and then I'd return to normal. Then I'd leave. The next day, I couldn't remember what I'd done.'

'You do remember, because you've given us all the details. What happened?'

'I didn't think about it any more.'

'It wasn't important?'

'No, that's right.'

'You told me that you used to cut articles out of the newspaper.'

'Yes.'

'Even about the murders you'd committed?'

'No, no.'

'You never cut out articles about your murders?'

'No.'

'Why not? Because in '84, for example, for the little girl in Pont-à-Mousson, there must have been articles in the papers.'

'Yes, I read the articles.'

'You read them? And you weren't scared?'

'No.'

'And the first one, did you forget it, or did it bother you for a long time?'

'I know that … it's true … it bothered me.'

Pont-à-Mousson, again … I wasn't sure if he was doing it on purpose to duck the conversation, but the mere mention of old cases reminded him of the crime. Then he would remember very precise episodes. He spoke of them spontaneously.

We continued our conversation. I told him that I didn't believe this was his first murder. He observed me.

'But the first time you killed, weren't you scared afterwards, even then?'

'Yes, I was scared.'

'The very first time, were you alone, all alone?'

'I was alone.'

'I know which one that was, and so do you.'

Francis Heaulme looked solemn and hunched up on his stool. I told him it no longer mattered. That I wasn't there for that. My investigation was over.

'I'd say it was a man, am I right?'

'Yeah, it was a man.'

'He was elderly, wasn't he?'

He nodded.

'You see, I've known it for a long time. You've been telling me about it for a long time. I haven't told anyone. I know the name of the first one.'

'Oh, I've forgotten ... It was a long time ago. I was a minor.'

Had Heaulme's former neighbour, 'Bouboule', been the first victim of his violent fantasies? I asked him when he had his second attack. Francis Heaulme replied:

'After my mother's death.'

'Is that what started it all?'

'That did it. I said to myself: I'm going to do someone in, I'm going to mangle someone.'

It was my last visit, and I didn't want to go back over the events. I decided to cut him short and ask one last question:

'I'd like to know what you feel when you're found out for committing a murder.'

'I don't feel anything at all,' he replied calmly, as if surprised at such a question.

Without warning, he changed the subject and started talking about the suicide of his cell mate. An ageing, sick and disabled man, convicted for vice, about whom he often used to say that death was the best thing that could happen to him. Once again, alarm bells started ringing. What was he playing at? Was he trying to tell me that it wasn't a suicide? Worse, that he had committed a fresh murder? And yet I had read the reports made at the time: there didn't seem to be any doubt.

It was definitely a suicide. I didn't want to get dragged into a new horror. I preferred to talk about other things with him. His brief love affairs, for example. He was afraid of women, and yet this problem had never affected his behaviour. It was not the trigger for his killer urges, alcohol was. Thinking of a couple of files I'd read in Rosny-sous-Bois, about crimes committed in public places, I asked him:

'Have you ever done anything in front of people?'

'When I want something, I want it, I take it. It's in my head.'

His tone was peremptory.

'At any price?'

'Yeah. When I want something, I get it.'

This man had no limits. He was unbelievably dangerous.

Before parting, I asked him if we would be battling against each other again at the next trial, as we had done in Quimper.

'We'll see,' he replied absently, and rose.

A brief goodbye and he was already in the doorway. Not another word, not a glance, not a gesture that was different from usual. This last visit was exactly like the first. And then suddenly, just before he went through the barred gate that would separate us for ever, he turned round and said:

'You'll see, François, we'll meet again. I know I'll always see you again!'

With a moment, he had disappeared before I could find a reply. Once again, he was getting away. Three years later, at Draguignan court of assizes, his behaviour confirmed that it was utterly impossible to find a chink in his armour.

13

Acquittal and life

In the following months, Francis Heaulme went from one court of assizes to another. I did not attend all these trials. In Metz, he was sentenced to life to run concurrently with an eighteen-year sentence for the murder of young Laurence Guillaume. Her cousin got twenty years in jail. There was one significant variant in the defendant's story: during the trial, Francis Heaulme declared that he 'was very fond of his father who had tried to help him'. This correction was more in keeping with the evidence gathered during the investigation.

Another piece of evidence regarding Francis Heaulme came to light. During a medical examination, the doctors detected Klinefelter's syndrome, a rare genetic anomaly. He had an extra sex chromosome, XXY instead of the usual male arrangement, XY. This was not without significance. Apart from a physical malformation which prevented him from having full sexual intercourse, his behaviour was affected by a feeling of inferiority and confusion in his sexual preferences. Clearly, for an investigator, that can explain the incomplete sexual nature of some crimes and the random choice of his victims, men or women. But the experts were categorical, this anomaly was not the cause of deviant behaviour. Francis Heaulme's judgement was not altered. It was not serial killer syndrome. Naturally, his counsel did not share this view.

In February 1994, the Bordeaux court of assizes delivered a verdict that took everyone by surprise. The case of the young conscript from Périgueux ended with an acquittal. The jury had not been able to decide between the two suspects identified in the initial police investigation and the two known criminals, Francis Heaulme and Didier G, charged by the gendarmes for the same crime. The lack of tangible proof, the witnesses' changing testimonies and the skilful arguments put forward by the seasoned defence counsels did not make it easy for them to reach a decision. Francis Heaulme says, not without irony, to anyone who will listen, that he still cannot understand the verdict. He was convinced he would be found guilty.

As time went by, I was involved in other investigations, tracking down other criminals. Heaulme gradually went out of my mind. The special unit had been disbanded after the end of the first trial in Quimper. A few departments were still sending in the odd request for assistance, but they were routinely refused, for the reason that I was no longer working on Francis Heaulme. My superiors were still the same and the subject remained taboo. Fortunately, however, as investigators are fond of working with direct contacts, some business can be dealt with over the phone. It was not until 1997 that Aline Pérès's killer came into my life again. In May, I received a summons to appear before the court of assizes in Draguignan.

Fate had it that this trial took place just as Belgium was reeling from the Marc Dutroux child murder case. There, child killers were in the headlines. Joris was a little Flemish boy and it was common knowledge that Francis Heaulme had been to Belgium. That was all it took for a swarm of foreign journalists to arrive and ask to meet me. I quickly reacquainted myself with the case. My colleagues from Aix-en-Provence confirmed that there had been no developments since Heaulme had been charged. Francis Heaulme had retracted his confession and the identity of his accomplice was still a mystery. Once again it was a complicated case, but, unlike the first trial, everyone was now familiar with Heaulme. It should be possible to nail him, as it was permitted to refer to all the cases that had been tried, and his retractions no longer worried me.

As I was about to leave Rennes for the Riviera, the commander of the criminal investigation unit insisted I travel to Draguignan by train. The south was paralysed by a railway strike and, more importantly, there was no station in Draguignan. I pointed this out, but he remained unmoved. I picked up his written order and kept it to add to my collection of idiocies. In the end, I drove down in my own car.

At the Draguignan gendarmerie, two colleagues were waiting for me to fine-tune our strategy and polish our testimonies. The local investigations would be referred to by the local investigators. The other investigations carried out by the criminal investigation unit would be kept completely separate. I would cover Heaulme's personality and behaviour during his last interview. The purpose of this division was to be as clear as possible at the trial and avoid misunderstandings. Each of us would deal with the aspect that he personally had handled, and could thus face the barrage of questions without floundering.

On 21 May 1997, at 9 a.m., we were outside the entrance of the Var Court of Assizes. These law courts were very different from those in Quimper.

The court room was vast and suffused with light. The bench was only slightly higher than the witness stand, and the plaintiffs' bench faced the dock. The atmosphere was not oppressive, it felt like a classroom. Francis Heaulme entered, flanked by two young police officers wearing black boilersuits and boots. Tall as ever, he was wearing his usual shapeless grey and white sweater over a bullet-proof vest that made him more rigid than usual. Restricted in his Kevlar straitjacket, he held himself bolt upright. His hands behind his back, he stood facing the parents of the child, who stared at him. Pursing his lips, he stared right back into their eyes.

Then came the time-honoured ritual of selecting the jury. The witnesses' roll-call was quick. They were all sent away until the next day, or even later, except for me. The presiding judge asked the usher to show me to a separate room, explaining that he would call me twice, that day to question me about Francis Heaulme's personality, and then at a later stage to testify as an investigator. Meanwhile, the defendant gazed attentively around the room. He stared at some of the witnesses, in particular the personnel from the Antibes hospital where he had been an in-patient at the time of the murder. The judge then addressed the defendant:

'Mr Heaulme, do you have anything to say before we begin?'

Mechanically, Healme replied:

'No, it's OK. I'm used to the courts by now.'

From his tone of voice, I could tell he was prepared to fight. During the morning of that first day of the trial, I remained alone in a room. From the window, I watched the life of a Provence market, and time plodded by. I learned later that when the details of the case were read out, the parents were distraught, but it was the young psychologist who was there to support them who left the court in tears. In this child murder case, it was obvious that Francis Heaulme had been aided by an accomplice, especially to reach the scene of the murder. Several other strands of the investigation pointed to the existence of an accomplice, but there was no proof and, so far, Heaulme had never revealed his name. The judge began his examination:

'Mr Heaulme, tell us what you were doing on the day of the murder.'

Heaulme replied in a clear, confident voice:

'I was at the La Fontonne hospital in Antibes. I played cards. Three patients cheated. I got into a fight. Some male nurses restrained me and I calmed down. Then in the afternoon, I drove to Grimaud with one of the male nurses. He had to book some bungalows for a hospital trip. I went along for the ride.'

The judge seized the opportunity:

'What's the name of this man, the one whose car you went in?'

Heaulme replied:

'I know his name, but I can't say it. He was in court this morning.'

The judge suggested a name and the defendant replied that it could be him. The examination continued painstakingly, then, abruptly, the mood changed. Francis Heaulme suddenly embarked on a new description of the murder scene:

'The kid wasn't dead. The man who was with me came back. He saw the kid. He said, "We've got to get rid of him." I said, "No, we should take him to hospital." The man wanted to hit me and added, "If you say anything, I'll kill you."'

In the room the tension rose. To avoid any kind of incident, the judge decided to suspend the examination briefly. He invited the mother of the young victim to take the witness stand. This step is often requested by the plaintiffs who want to tell the court of their suffering. Everyone dreads these moments, as they often lead to emotional outbursts. The tension rose even higher. A slim young woman dressed in white with dark circles under her red eyes entered the witness box. The mother of little Joris was holding three sheets of paper which she began to read slowly, with a slight accent:

'Your Honour, ladies and gentlemen of the jury. For months I have known that as soon as the accused entered the court room

I would turn to gaze at his hands. Those hands that killed my child in cold blood. It was a shock: those thin hands were hands that should build, not destroy. But it is in thought and mind that wickedness and perversity exist. Why, why? It is a question to which we will never have an answer. That question will haunt us all our lives. Lives that have been utterly shattered, that will never be as they were before.'

After a long pause for breath, she continued:

'Eight years ago, we were a very happy little family. Steven was fifteen, and Joris nine. Since that 5 April, our day-to-day life has been a constant battle against emptiness, despair, helplessness and the absurdity of Joris's death. Joris had barely started his life, life which he loved so much. He had everything to hope for, his future belonged to him. He was like a sparkling stream, running over waterfalls and rapids from time to time. Sadly, that stream will never reach the sea.'

Joris's mother paused. She looked exhausted. But then she continued:

'Can you imagine what Joris must have suffered that terrible night! Discovering new things was his passion. But in pursuing his exploration of life, which was just beginning for him, he was unlucky. That life was brutally taken from him, in such a cowardly manner.'

She looked at the jury, and then at the court, and went on:

'We know that Francis Heaulme had an accomplice and that he cannot be found. To him, I wish to say this: I do not understand how you can live with such a secret. I know that sooner or later you will be punished, if only by your conscience which

233

must be tormenting you. If you have children, are you able to look them in the eyes?'

Then, slowly, she turned to Francis Heaulme.

'And to the accused, I want to say this: you adored your mother. Luckily for her, she is dead and I'm glad, glad that she does not have to go through this. I pity her, because for a mother, it is appalling to learn that one's child is capable of killing human beings, an innocent child. It is high time for the accused to be convicted. For eight years, he has dominated our lives, he's been pulling the strings. Ladies and gentlemen of the jury, a few years ago, France passed a law on the appropriate sentence for child murderers. Apply it! Your Honour, in the name of all the accused's victims, for the sake of their families and especially in the name of Joris, I beg you, ensure that this man receives proper psychological help in prison, that he receives proper treatment so that he never does this again. He must be prevented from creating further victims at all costs. (...) For us, it is already too late. The accused gave Joris the death sentence, and he gave us, Joris's father, mother and brother, a life sentence. We have to go on living with a grief that is almost unbearable, with a shadow that will hang over us for ever, with Joris beside us. My husband and I have never known hatred, but our struggle is to prevent other parents from experiencing the same hell. Your Honour, ladies and gentlemen of the jury, we beg you to take this into account when you pronounce your verdict.'

Soundlessly, the woman went back to her seat. Some jurors had tears in their eyes, as did many other people in the room.

The judge was quick to seize the moment and turned to Francis Heaulme:

'You must tell her who was with you. Tell her, Mr Heaulme!'

Impassive, he replied:

'It was Mr B. His car was a blue Fiat. If I denied it was him, it was because he threatened to kill me.'

There was a murmur of utter disbelief. B, one of the nurses at the hospital summonsed to appear, was scheduled to testify the next day.

The psychologists and psychiatrists then gave evidence. Their reports were similar to the previous ones. One of the doctors did, however, describe Heaulme's intelligence as borderline. The expert mentioned Klinefelter's syndrome. He spoke of a chromosomal abnormality, and expounded at length. The defence tried to use the information. According to the counsel, it was more than likely that this anomaly was at the root of his client's pathological behaviour. As far as he was concerned, Heaulme could not be considered normal and, from that point of view, he could also not be deemed responsible for his actions. The expert refused to endorse this theory.

When the usher showed me to the witness box, I knew nothing of what had just transpired. I was more relaxed than at the Quimper trial. Heaulme was serving a long sentence, and whatever happened here he was not about to be released. During my testimony, I went over the various cases in which the accused had been involved, and mentioned the changes in his behaviour. I explained that he changed his tune according to his interlocutors and went from the haziest initial version to conclude with the utmost precision.

'How did he behave with regard to the case we are concerned with?' asked the judge.

'He is manipulative. He knows the name of the person who was with him on the day of the murder, but he won't say. It would backfire against him. It is the first time he's been tried for the murder of a child. He doesn't want to admit the inadmissible.'

Heaulme did not take his eyes off me, but he remained inscrutable. Nobody commented. That first day also saw an intervention by Pierre Gonzalez de Gaspard, who asked for the trial to be postponed. He wanted an order for further information to be gathered so as to identify the second man. However the judge ruled that the trial would continue.

The next day, everyone was impatient to see the male nurse accused by Francis Heaulme take his place on the witness stand, even though he had been cleared during the initial investigation. The eagerly awaited confrontation came to an abrupt close, however.

The judge called upon several members of the Antibes hospital team. He organised an impromptu identity parade. He placed the six witnesses facing the accused. They worked closely together and were visibly stressed, looking at each other in embarrassment.

'Is your accomplice one of the people you see before you, Mr Heaulme?' asked the judge.

'Yes!' he replied without hesitation, and he pointed at one of the male nurses. 'It's him!' he added.

Distraught, the man remained alone on the witness stand. His nervousness was palpable.

'But Mr Heaulme, this is not the same person whose name you gave yesterday!' commented the judge.

There was a general murmur. A few moments later, the supposed accomplice was cleared by the evidence of the investigation.

'But I'm telling you, my accomplice is here, in the room,' insisted Francis Heaulme.

There was turmoil. Exasperation was at its peak. Amid the commotion, a second identity parade was arranged. A second person was identified. Once again, confronted with the facts, the man singled out proved not to be the elusive accomplice. This absurd situation did not seem to bother Francis Heaulme, quite the opposite. Indifferent, he announced:

'I don't know now, I can't remember any more.'

The judge gave up in the end. It was the turn of my two colleagues and myself to testify, one after the other. We went over the countless details that he had given us. We explained how he had talked about a 'tree that went all limp', then described the scene of the crime and the murder itself with extreme precision. During my first colleague's testimony, Francis Heaulme permitted himself to make an extraordinary remark concerning the number of stab wounds the child had received from the screwdriver. In his most chilling tone, he said:

'It wasn't eighty-four stabbings, it was eighty-three.'

Those in the room could barely contain themselves. By the time we had finished testifying, Francis Heaulme could no longer deny his involvement in the murder. I went back to my seat in the court room. I wanted to listen to the rest of the trial, especially the testimonies of the hospital managers.

The judge examined them at length. Like many others, he found it hard to understand why no action had been taken by the medical team when Francis Heaulme had returned on the night of the murder. Had Heaulme not proclaimed to anyone who would listen: 'I've killed, I've killed!'? But he came up against a single reply, voiced by doctors and nurses alike: 'patient confidentiality'. There was nothing to be done, the judge himself could not break the law.

We would never find out, nor would we know why the log book of the car that Francis Heaulme claimed to have driven in with a member of the hospital staff was the only one that could not be found. One of my colleagues and I had an idea who Francis Heaulme's accomplice might be. During the investigation, we did not have the evidence we needed to pin him down. He was visibly afraid. His eyes avoided ours. Our gazes did not meet for a second. I could not help thinking about the horrific murder he had allowed to happen.

I also realised that Francis Heaulme had scaled new heights. In the absence of a specific interlocutor at the trial, he was amusing himself by playing games with the witnesses and the magistrates.

He had realised that solely the one particular crime was being dealt with, whereas it could only be understood in an overall context. Heaulme did his utmost to baffle and confuse. Besides, had he not warned us when he had stated he was 'used to the courts'?

The Draguignan jury was not out for long, and the sentence was the harshest Francis Heaulme had ever received: life imprisonment with a minimum of thirty years.

As I left the court room, the young victim's mother came up to me.

'I want to give you my testimony,' she said, holding out the three sheets.

Touched by her gesture, I was at a loss for words. She turned on her heel and left at once, exhausted, supported by her husband who was equally drained. They walked past several members of the hospital team from Antibes. Their expressions betrayed a similar exhaustion. Their encounter with the accused would doubtless scar them for life, with the terrible knowledge that would stay with them for a long time: Francis Heaulme's accomplice had succeeded in evading justice.

14

The cycle ride

November 1997. That autumn morning, I was a long way from imagining the storm that would be unleashed by my opening an envelope that lay among my other work correspondence. A few lines written on the letterhead of a Paris law firm, signed by Maître Estelle Dubois, outlined a case that had been in the news. She stated that a sixteen-year-old boy, Patrick Dils, had confessed to a crime which he subsequently denied. Ever since, he had dubbed himself 'the misunderstood innocent'.

At first glance, it seemed to be a simple request from a defence counsel, convinced of the innocence of her client who had been sentenced in January 1989 for a double child murder. She was writing to me because she had a keen interest in Francis Heaulme. The way in which these children had been killed bore an uncanny resemblance to the method of the serial killer, at least from what she had read in the press. In a few sentences, the lawyer described the crime: two children bludgeoned to death, found one Sunday on a footpath beside a railway line in Montigny-lès-Metz. Had Francis Heaulme been there or in the vicinity on the day the children were murdered, by any chance? The date was 28 September 1986.

The question perplexed me. I recalled that day in 1992 when, in Brest prison, I had had to stop Francis Heaulme when he was telling, one after the other, his 'little stories'. They all matched recognised homicides, except one. This one was about a bicycle ride. I could still remember every word.

A long time ago, on a Sunday, I was cycling down a street. It was in eastern France. There were some houses on the left. On the right there was an embankment and a railway line. Two kids threw stones at me when I rode past. At the end of the street there was a stop sign, a bridge and some dustbins. I left. When I came back later, I saw the kids' dead bodies near some railway carriages. There were also police and some firemen.

At the time, it had not been possible to link this to any case. Intrigued, I decided to check Frances Heaulme's itinerary that we had pieced together. With surprise, I noted that he had been in the area of Montigny-lès-Metz at the time.

Perhaps this was no mere coincidence after all. In any case, there wasn't enough evidence to draw any conclusions. But this little incident did tie up. Supposing I hadn't looked in the right place? Once again I checked the database of unsolved cases. There was nothing resembling this double murder. Nothing.

There was nothing even remotely similar. Consequently, it was not a common type of crime.

Then I worked backwards: carrying out a computer search for solved crimes concerning children beside railway lines. I only found one result. The printout was brief. It listed the key features of the double murder at Montigny-lès-Metz. The places described by Francis Heaulme corresponded exactly to the scene of the murder. It would appear that the killer had been describing this place, and these victims.

Then I thought about all the transpositions he continually made during our conversations. As he did with Bouboule, to whom he attributed different roles according to different cases. In the Joris Viville case, Heaulme spoke to me about 'a child who had thrown stones at him after having shouted abuse'. We knew that it hadn't been the young Belgian boy, so whom was he talking about? This revelation had been so important that a helicopter search was organised to find places with dustbins and a bridge, where Joris might have been killed. At the time, no place corresponding to this description had been discovered, and no wonder ...

Another detail came back to mind. When he was being interviewed in the Var, in the south, Francis Heaulme said he had met a nurse from Montigny-lès-Metz at the hospital in Antibes. That was not true. What had he really meant, given that there was nothing random about his lies? ... The link between his little story and this double murder now seemed obvious, but what on earth was I to do with these clues? The Montigny-lès-Metz case had been tried. Replying to this letter would, implicitly, call the verdict into question. Could Patrick Dils, the youngest person to be sentenced for life, be the victim of a miscarriage of justice? And, at the heart of the grisly affair, Francis Heaulme, once more a child-killer? It was a huge challenge and I was conscious of the repercussions that my decision would have, but I had no other choice. These doubts must be removed.

I discussed it with my immediate superiors. Fortunately, the leadership of the Rennes criminal investigation unit had changed a few months previously. However, the problem I raised caused a stir. Several months went by. The report I had given to my divisional head to pass on to the Metz prosecutor lay forgotten on a corner of his desk.

Despite my inquiries, nobody seemed to know what had happened to this document. Had it been passed on to the prosecutor or not? Nobody knew ... In any case, the press got wind of it and whipped up a furore. Most of the papers talked about the loss of a mysterious report written by a gendarme from Rennes. This document could call into question the conviction of Patrick Dils for the double murder in Montigny-lès-Metz. I was aghast. Two days later, the report arrived at the Metz court, surprisingly via that of Brest. It had taken three months to reach its destination.

Coincidence or not, Patrick Dils's lawyers seized the document and immediately lodged an appeal. As a result, in January 1998 I found myself in Paris, in the chambers of senior legal counsel. This highly experienced magistrate was heading the investigations for the retrial. It was unusual for a criminal investigation officer to be summoned at this level. I was given a very formal reception. I thought I would have to go over Francis Heaulme's behaviour during the years of investigations point by point in order to explain the reasons for my report. But the conversation did not go along these lines at all. The senior magistrate was aloof, almost severe. Then, by way of introduction to the question of my report, he said:

'Just because some madman talks nonsense, that's no reason to write nonsense.'

I was speechless. I didn't know what he was driving at. Was it because of the media pressure, the complications that an appeal entailed? I replied:

'First of all, Francis Heaulme is not mad. He has been examined by psychiatrists, there have been second opinions and third opinions ad infinitum. Secondly, what he says always matches up with something he has done. His words are not to be taken lightly.'

Thus began an interview that was tense, to say the least. Nearly three hours later, when I left the Paris Law Courts, I felt as though I was emerging from an examination and I didn't know whether I had passed or failed. But the main thing was that I had said everything there was to be said about Heaulme's character. I was to be summoned again to finalise my report. The senior magistrate's attitude was doubtless dictated by caution because of the high stakes. He probably wanted to assess my credibility and check personally some of the points raised.

A month later, I was back under the gilded portals of the Court of Appeal. The grilling I received was just as ruthless.

From various things he said, I gathered that the senior magistrate intended to interview Francis Heaulme himself.

I pictured the meeting of these two diametrically opposite men, and I feared that not much of any use would come of it. As I was about to sign my interview, I decided to ask a question:

'Do you know whether the Montigny-lès-Metz victims were throwing stones at passers-by?'

It was the clerk who replied:

'Yes, there are testimonies that mention it.'

That confirmed that Francis Heaulme had indeed seen the boys. This detail had not been mentioned in the police messages or in the newspaper reports at the time. A few weeks later, Francis Heaulme was interviewed.

Patrick Dils's defence counsel informed the press. The headlines talked of the biggest miscarriage of justice of the century. This new development soon made the Metz killer front-page news again. That was how I found out that Heaulme had confirmed the contents of the report to the magistrate of the review panel. Better still, he had provided further information, in particular, how he had been dressed on the day of the murder, and who his friends were at the time. Always with the same attention to detail.

Further investigations were necessary. The matter was put into the hands of the Nancy police. I kept my head down and passed on my information. Like everybody else, I learned how the investigation was progressing via the press.

The man in charge of the investigation was no other than André M. This experienced police commander had been the head of the Pont-à-Mousson investigation. Francis Heaulme's unpredictable behaviour and the variations in his accounts did not surprise him. The police chief once again used the device of the sketch, and Heaulme complied. André M was fully aware of its importance. He in his turn gathered valuable information about the presence of the serial killer in Montigny. Heaulme confirmed that he had seen the victims but swore he had done nothing to them.

For reasons that I do not know, the judicial authorities ordered a change of team in spring 1999. It was the turn of the Metz gendarmerie to take over the case. Francis Heaulme then encountered Pedro again, an old acquaintance. He added to his initial diagrams, giving the police precise details, in particular a path that led to the victims' bodies and which nobody had mentioned before.

On 3 April 2001, the Court of Appeal announced the closure of the investigation and ordered Patrick Dils's sentence to be quashed and a retrial to be held at a different court of assizes. The presence of Francis Heaulme at the scene of the crime on the day of the murder was sufficient for the former verdict to be deemed unsafe. Meanwhile, I had left the gendarmerie, but that did not prevent me from being called as a witness at Patrick Dils's retrial. On 20 June 2001 I found myself in Reims, on the witness stand at the Marne region juvenile court of assizes. Once again, Patrick Dils stood before a jury.

The man who entered the dock was no longer the shy adolescent described by the press of the time. Patrick Dils had spent more than half his life in prison, and yet he had maintained a reticent air. I could tell he was extremely tense. He looked a little awkward in his navy blue blazer that looked a little too big for him. I later found out that it had been lent to him at the last minute by one of his lawyers.

As the names of the witnesses and their order of appearance were read out, I felt that this was like a repeat of the trial of fifteen years earlier. I also knew that the investigation was not completely over. As it happened, new witnesses came forward after the verdict.

I was surprised by another aspect of the situation. Paradoxically, Francis Heaulme and I were there as simple witnesses. He was not the defendant and I was not the investigator. I would not meet him at any point during the six days of the trial, which was held in camera. I knew that Heaulme was in Montigny-lès-Metz on 28 September 1986, that he saw the boys and their lifeless bodies. I felt as if I were in a topsy-turvy world, that this was the wrong trial. I was off topic: it was Dils who was on trial, and I was talking about Heaulme.

On the witness stand, however, I endeavoured to explain who Francis Heaulme really was. I stressed the many similarities between his crimes and this double homicide, but I felt as though I was talking in a vacuum. My words seemed to ring hollow. Visibly, they were irrelevant to this trial. Even the murder of Annick Maurice, in Metz, only a month after this one, did not raise any questions.

Then it was Heaulme's turn to take the stand. I did not attend his cross-examination. I waited in the witnesses' room, in case I was needed.

I learned what he had said from the newspapers. Reading the different reports, I noted that he was actually delighted with the situation. This time, he had a made-to-measure role, he who had always claimed only to be a spectator to the crimes he had committed. On the witness stand, Francis Heaulme took care firstly to address the family of one of the victims. Without the hint of a smile, he stated:

'I give you my word as a man that I did not kill your son.'

Then he addressed the judge:

'I cannot be the author of this double crime, because I am religious. Besides, when I kill, I kiss my victims on the forehead.'

I knew he was making things up. Without presuming to question the genuineness of his conversion, I knew that his interest in religion went back to 1991, when he had met his girl-friend in Alsace, not before. As for the kisses on his victims' fore-heads, this was the first I had heard of it. It was an intriguing twist, why had he admitted to it? Wasn't this revelation, on the contrary, a veiled confession? That of a man who knew, and with good reason, that that strange gesture would have been impossible on these children because of their injuries?

In another little remark reported in the press, Heaulme declared to the judge, by way of a conclusion:

'It wasn't me who killed those children, but I don't think it was Patrick Dils either.'

Heaulme had given his opinion like an expert. Just before leaving the witness stand, he took the liberty of wishing the defendant good luck. Naively, Patrick Dils thanked him. I found this cruelly ironic.

Most people had been expecting earth-shattering revelations, a public confession. Little did they know Heaulme. A lot of journalists talked of a 'non-event'. There was huge disappointment. Even so, I hoped that my testimony had been clear enough for the jury to have grasped what was hidden behind Heaulme's mask of respectability. The counsel for the prosecution called for an acquittal, but a few hours later the verdict came. Patrick Dils was convicted again: twenty-five years imprisonment. All the hopes of Patrick Dils and his family were suddenly dashed, all those wounds had been reopened for nothing.

The defendant immediately appealed against this decision. A year went by and the case was in the news again. In April 2002, the Lyon court of assizes was invaded by a horde of journalists and people avid to gain access at last to all the pieces of this puzzle, since the law did not insist on the trial being held in camera. This third trial was exceptional in that it was to last for two weeks.

Two versions of the truth were being presented: the confessions of the accused, which he later retracted, and the physical presence of a known killer at the scene of the crime. The courts had therefore ordered a further investigation. For a year, the Metz criminal investigators had explored every possible avenue. The initial investigation that incriminated Patrick Dils had been put under the microscope. No detail was overlooked. Some new elements, both in his favour and against him, had been included. At the same time, Francis Heaulme had been questioned again and his stories checked. Witnesses had been found, some of whom had been in the vicinity of the crime scene. The quest for truth was paramount. The presiding judge of the Lyon court of assizes passed all this evidence to all the parties concerned. This new trial was therefore different from the previous two.

The first days of the trial were devoted to studying the personality of the defendant, the crime, the investigative techniques used and the charges against him. Exceptionally, the jurors took an active part in the proceedings, so that notes were being passed round on either side of the judge. They contained unanswered questions. This determination to uncover the truth about the murder of 28 September 1986 was gruelling for the victims' families, who once more had to lay bare their suffering in public. The counsel for the prosecution was the first to raise the fundamental problems. He pointed out to the police officer in charge of the case that the window of time when Patrick Dils would have had the opportunity to act was extremely narrow. He challenged the police's conviction:

'In ten minutes, he would really have to have had a very strong motive! I've been working in the court of assizes for twenty years, and usually there's an identifiable motive. In this case, there isn't.'

He pointed out inconsistencies in Patrick Dils's explanations which lacked coherence. He stressed the failure to follow up vital leads, like the witness who had mentioned passing a man covered in blood who was not the accused. Lastly, he noted that Patrick Dils had not revealed anything that would only have been known to the murderer, contrary to what the former inspector had claimed. Furthermore, at no time had mention been made of the fact that one of the victims' underpants had been pulled down, a detail described by Francis Heaulme. To conclude, the counsel for the prosecution read the very detailed statement of another suspect, questioned a few weeks before Patrick Dils, who also, astonishingly, had confessed to the double murder. So Dils was not the only one. The man's name was Henri L. Like Henri L, Francis Heaulme's imaginary friend on Moulin Blanc beach …

The flaws in the initial investigation had been revealed. Despite everything, the doubts as to Patrick Dils's guilt had not been completely dispelled. In the court room, many people were waiting for the proof, the decisive piece of evidence.

The witnesses succeeded each other on the stand and the atmosphere changed depending on whether they strengthened the prosecution's case or that of the defence. At the end of the first week of the trial, opinions were divided as to whether the defendant was guilty or not. At last the moment came for my testimony. The judge had ensured that I would be the last witness. That way, she said, 'we'll have plenty of time to listen to you'. Her tone, bordering on the maternal, was soothing, but behind this approach was all the power of an experienced magistrate who knew the case inside out and was aware of the limits of human actions.

'The court is gathered here today, we could say, because of you, because of the report you wrote. So, Mr Abgrall, what have you got to tell us?'

It was a solemn moment. The things I was going to talk about had no bearing on the defendant. Everybody was waiting. They must all have the chance to evaluate the credibility of Francis Heaulme's declarations and must have the key to understanding the character who would be facing them the next day. Explaining this man's psychology clearly was no easy matter.

Slowly I retraced the Moulin Blanc investigation and my meetings with Francis Heaulme. I mentioned the similarities between the murders, his presence at the scene of the crime, the little stories he told me in prison, his gruesome dreams, the transpositions, Bouboule, the interview protocols, the taboo words, the importance of the sketches, the special unit ... I tried not to omit anything, so as to show that despite the apparent complexity, Heaulme actually operated in a very straightforward manner. Francis Heaulme was telling a single, unique story, that of his journey, in which he mixed up all his murders. Any interpretation only made sense if you looked at the whole picture. I pointed out the recurrent elements of his testimonies. In each case, he saw the victims alive, then witnessed them being attacked. He tried to intervene and prevent 'the other' and sometimes killed. He always presented himself as the good guy. If he did admit to the crime, it was only momentarily, then he retracted his confession. His confessions were of no importance in themselves. The only thing that counted were the verifiable clues he provided.

More than three hours went by. The jurors kept passing notes around, questions were fired from all sides. The judge invited me to give my analysis of the Montigny case. I highlighted the similarities between the names: a Henri L at Moulin Blanc, another at Montigny-lès-Metz. The instance of the anglers who took the witness stand, who had given a blood-spattered Francis Heaulme a lift in their Renault 4 on the day of the murder, and those in the Joris case who were non-existent.

The lawyers then cross-examined me. The counsel for the plaintiffs criticised the notion of Francis Heaulme having a 'signature', underlined by the double murder in Montigny-lès-Metz. And yet there was nothing random in the way the murderer selected his victims and operated. His choices, conscious or otherwise, were tantamount to a signature, on a par with a fingerprint. It was necessary to use other means of deciphering a crime scene. The signature was also apparent in the way Heaulme talked about the murder, in the omissions or the arrangement of his memories. This was another way in which Francis Heaulme and his accomplices had been caught.

On 16 April at 9 a.m., Captain H and Chief Thierry P from the Metz criminal investigation unit took the witness stand. These investigators had been in charge of gathering further information and reviewing the initial investigation. They gave a slide presentation showing the chronology and the positions of the witnesses. Each witness, on the afternoon of the murder, was shown on a large panel moving forward on the map of the district. It was clear that the last sighting of the young victims was around 5.15 p.m. At 6.30 p.m., members of their families started looking for them. At that time, Patrick Dils was still away for the weekend with his parents. Captain H gave a report on his additional investigations. He stated that Francis Heaulme had given some details of this crime and that he had checked a number of points in the original file. This had led him to doubt Patrick Dils's involvement in the murder. The importance of their testimonies was such that they were subjected to a barrage of questions. Captain H did not leave the court of assizes until 9 p.m.

On 17 April, at 2 p.m., when Francis Heaulme appeared, our eyes met. Unusually, he had difficulty sustaining my gaze. Thinner, and visibly very weak, he no longer resembled the Heaulme that I knew. His salt-and-pepper hair had been shaved, which made him look like an old man. Wearing his usual grey sweater, he looked lost. When he walked past me, I noticed that he was trying to work out where he was. He did not seem his normal self. Then, shortly after he had begun to speak, he asked if he could sit down. He explained that he was on medication for phlebitis.

Invited by the judge to describe what he had seen on 28 September 1986, Francis Heaulme declared:

'If I had killed the kids, I'd have said so in Reims. I don't want to confess to a murder I did not commit. That wasn't me. It's not my style. I use an Opinel and I strangle with my bare hands.'

A long murmur ran around the court. The examination lasted for two hours, during which Francis Heaulme claimed to have lied to the gendarmes, then he retreated behind his contradictions. He didn't want to take the rap he said. However, he added that he had thought a lot about Patrick Dils, and said: 'I don't think it was him. He's too young.'

This was going nowhere. Suddenly, Francis Heaulme started talking about another murder:

'I've always admitted the murders I did. I do care about the families, I do feel remorse. There was a business in the south, at Juan-les-Pins, the Joris Viville case. That kid I did strangle and there was another man with me, a nurse (*he gave the name*). He put the boy in the pine wood, he was the one who finished him off. He said to me afterwards that if I said anything, he would kill me. When I appeared in court, they had an identity parade. I didn't say anything, but he was there.'

The expressions on some of the jurors' faces changed. They had just understood. Francis Heaulme always gave additional information, but about another case. His appearance came to an end shortly afterwards.

The next day, the defence speeches of the three lawyers for the plaintiffs – the victims' families – turned into indictments against Patrick Dils. Their conviction did not seem to have been shaken by all the testimonies and evidence presented. They tried to wipe the Francis Heaulme episode out of the jury's minds by insisting on the precision of the accused's confessions. As regards the serial killer, they called him a 'substitute culprit'.

The counsel for the prosecution's closing speech summed up the case:

'Everything seems dubious to me. I don't know whether Patrick Dils's confessions relate to a criminal act or are pure fantasy.'

He stressed the 'irregularities' in the initial investigation and the way the law had been stretched. Then he raised the issue of Francis Heaulme.

'Heaulme is not a bolt out of the blue. We have to recognise that if the investigators at the time had known about him, they would have followed the Heaulme lead very closely ... He has always confirmed his presence in Rue Vénizélos. He is astonishingly familiar with the scene of the crime, which he describes in perfect detail ... This man saw the two boys with their heads crushed before anybody else, and one of them had his trousers down.'

He repeated Healme's statement that this was not his usual way of operating, which was strangling bare-handed or stabbing with an Opinel knife.

'He professes the sordid to protect himself from the horrific, that is Francis Heaulme's true style.'

He then spoke about the limitations of the scenario outlined by the original prosecution against Patrick Dils. He did not believe a psychologist's interpretation that imputed his acting out of his fantasies to the 'pressure cooker' effect, an explosion of sudden violence that is undetectable and does not repeat itself. As far as he was concerned, nothing had been established beyond a doubt in this case. Finally he addressed the defendant:

'If you benefit from the fact that there is the shadow of a doubt, please have the grace to keep your head down. You have taken the place of the murderer, don't now try and take that of the victims. You have only been a victim of yourself.'

The prosecutor did not call for a sentence.

The roles of the two defence counsels had already been allocated. Maître Becker came in first, and his job was to highlight the inconsistencies in the initial investigation, the infringements of the defendant's rights. He evoked the similarities between the confessions received from two other men. This was disturbing. He emphasised the fragility of his client in 1986, an immature adolescent, incapable of having committed this crime which he had constantly denied since. He had never believed that his client was guilty. In a similar vein, the second counsel, Maître Florand, pointed out the holes in the case. He wondered about the likelihood of Francis Heaulme arriving at the scene of a murder of which he was not the author. He stressed the implausibility of Patrick Dils's confession and questioned the competence of the head of the investigation at the time.

And finally, it was the defendant who had the last word. He addressed the bench, and then the families:

'I'm not the sort of person who climbs onto the prison roof to shout and scream. I am Patrick Dils and Patrick Dils does not do that. I am sorry to have caused you suffering through my lies and my behaviour. I never wanted to cause anybody pain. I am innocent. I did not take the lives of your children.'

It was 8.30 p.m., on 24 April 2002, when the acquittal was announced. A clamour of joy greeted the verdict. The judge asked the public to be quiet as she felt the noise was unseemly. The victims' families were devastated, and their lawyers tried to console them. The grandmother of one of the boys made it clear that she still believed Dils was guilty. Meanwhile, Patrick Dils quietly wept, then regained his composure. The defence counsels were delighted. The defendant's father erupted with joy in his wife's arms. We knew that a major event had just occurred. Everything happened very fast. The court room emptied in a joyful commotion. The counsel for the prosecution observed the scene, with a broad smile.

I felt a surge of profound relief. It was a brave verdict. I now knew that Francis Heaulme's 'dreams' had been understood.

Afterword

Quite unintentionally, Francis Heaulme had often revealed the failings of the legal and medical institutions. For years, this man from nowhere had left a trail of victims behind him unhindered. How had such a simple soul – 'with a deranged mind' as he had so often been described in the press – been able to slip through the net so easily? What kind of system allows a dangerous individual to stay in dozens of psychiatric establishments and then blithely to continue as before? Why had our investigative techniques not enabled us to arrest him sooner? Was prison really the right place for him?

Of course, we can argue that these cases happened some time ago, and it is always easy to criticise with hindsight. These days, patient confidentiality is so sacrosanct that witnesses say nothing, or very little. If medical records are not available, there is no proper follow-up for patients who are constantly on the move.

Thus, vast amounts of information constituting an important indicator of a person's dangerousness remain buried, as there is no cross-referencing. A new file is opened for each new patient arriving in a medical establishment. It contains details of their current problem, but remains for ever silent after the patient's departure. That way the legal and the medical never mix. A pity, especially when the expert psychiatrists and psychologists appointed by the courts then refer, in the court of assizes, to the dangerousness of the defendant. How many people were aware of it before they come to the attention of the law?

As for the investigation techniques used, I recognise that they were sometimes primitive. These days, a person's criminal career can only be legally retraced through their convictions. Hence, if the person does not have a criminal record, we know nothing, or almost nothing. For crimes displaying a practice, or a criminal signature, the evidence showing that the act is purely a repetition remains dispersed. Each investigator works on one crime and cannot go beyond. The investigating magistrate is obstructed by this same rule. And yet, the systematic drawing up and checking of a suspect's background would make it possible to identify a criminal path, an itinerary ... Maybe we'll achieve this one day.

Fortunately, real scientific and technical advances have been made. There are countless reliable investigation procedures and means of gathering proof, DNA fingerprints being a prime example. These are left by everybody, all the time. It is enough to touch an item of clothing, lick a stamp, lose a hair or hold a book to enable a DNA sample to be taken. Even though the

DNA database is restricted to certain categories of delinquents and criminals, it provides valuable information. This is definitely a plus.

On another level, databases have been improved. Information technology, combined with a more comprehensive inputting of the parameters of a case, has led to more efficient cross-referencing and the identification of similarities between cases. It has become routine to carry out a criminal analysis on major cases, and this has brought to light other serial killer cases.

However, that is not enough. Investigators are aware that there is a lack of training in criminal psychology. Each criminal investigation officer is ready to look for the proof, that concrete element that reassures and physically proves that somebody has committed a crime, but when that proof is lacking, there are only witness statements and suspects. That is where it becomes necessary to draw on different disciplines. How is it possible to understand and expose an individual's actions through questioning and traditional approaches when that person is in a different world? We need other tools. The interpretation of a criminal situation, analysing a person's speech – everything has to be measured differently. They are often full of invisible clues for the investigator or the magistrate who will sometimes discern these without being able to name them. That is what some people call 'instinct' or 'having a nose'. For example, the place chosen by the murderer, the victim ... these are all clues related to the suspect's personality. This information is available to the investigator, but it is not necessarily picked up. Psychological and other approaches are even more important in missing persons investigations. If homicide is suspected, the absence of a body makes it impossible to establish links between modes of operation, so where does one begin? These needs became apparent when the institution started to bring in private criminologists or psychologists. Nowadays, things are changing. Some psychologists have been taken on by police and gendarme training colleges, and Rennes university has set up an Institute of Criminology which is open to investigators from different bodies, magistrates and expert psychologists who are trained in analysing criminal situations. The multidisciplinary approach and the exchange of expertise, without replacing the traditional investigation, will certainly thwart criminal careers like that of Francis Heaulme. It is foreseeable that this type of teaching will be directly integrated in the training of all those involved in criminal investigations.

Today, I have moved on. And yet there is a question I still ask myself: is prison really the right place for Francis Heaulme?

Jean-François Abgrall can be contacted at www.abgrall-jf.com